Patsy Westcott

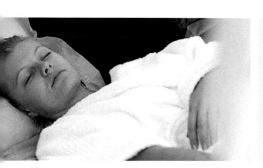

Healthy Heart

Recipes and Advice for a Healthier Heart

food solutions

TED SMART

Healthy Heart

Recipes and Advice for a Healthier Heart

food solutions

Executive Editor – Jane McIntosh
Editor – Trevor Davies
Executive Art Editor – Leigh Jones
Book Design – Birgit Eggers
Picture Research – Christine
    Junemann
Production – Lucy Woodhead

First published in Great Britain in 2001
by Hamlyn, an imprint of
Octopus Publishing Group Limited,
2–4 Heron Quays, London E14 4JP

Copyright © Octopus Publishing
Group Limited 2001
ISBN 600 60627 9

This edition produced for
The Book People Ltd,
Hall Wood Avenue,
Haydock,
St Helens WA11 9UL

A catalogue record for this book is
available from the British Library

Printed in China

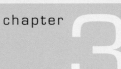

contents

LEFT: From the beginning to the end of your life a strong, healthy heart is necessary to help you live it to the full.

Heart disease is **a major killer worldwide**, especially in developed countries where people eat high-fat, low-fibre Western diets.

In the United Kingdom, which has one of the highest levels of heart disease in the world, there are 300,000 heart attacks every year, about half of which are fatal. Meanwhile, a further 1.4 million people suffer from angina, the main symptom of coronary heart disease. It is surely no coincidence that **many of the people who die from heart disease live in countries where diets are high in saturated fats and low in fresh fruits and vegetables**.

The good news is that **the death toll from heart disease can be substantially reduced by eating a healthy diet**. Many studies have shown this over the years, from big population studies begun in the 1960s, showing that people living in countries around the Mediterranean have lower levels of heart disease and death from heart disease, to the ever-increasing number of more recent studies focusing on the beneficial effects of antioxidant vitamins and minerals found in fresh fruit and vegetables. Other studies have shown the benefits of foods such as oily fish, olive oil and nutrients found in nuts and seeds.

In fact, over the past couple of decades an overwhelming amount of evidence has accumulated to show that a diet high in fresh fruit and vegetables, oily fish, nuts and seeds, and wholegrain cereals **can actively help to prevent atherosclerosis**, the narrowing of the arteries that causes heart attacks and angina.

Of course, heart disease is not caused or prevented by any single factor, and even diet, important though it is, is not enough on its own to protect against heart disease. The aim of this book is to increase your **understanding of the many different factors that play a part in causing heart disease**.

The book begins by outlining the structure and function of the heart and blood vessels **and explaining what can go wrong.**

In Chapter 2, you will find details about the various **risk factors that can contribute to someone developing heart disease.** Although the mechanisms by which these increase the development of heart disease

RIGHT: Staying active is one of the secrets to gaining and maintaining a strong, healthy heart.

FAR RIGHT: Making good food choices is an important part of ensuring your heart and circulation stay healthy.

are still the subject of much scientific study and investigation, there is general agreement among experts on what they are and what can be done to minimize their impact.

In Chapter 3, there is practical, achievable advice on the **things you can do yourself to minimize the various risk factors** that may apply to you, including tips on how to handle stress and other lifestyle factors that may play a part in aggravating heart disease.

Chapter 4 contains clear information about the **huge range of drugs** designed to prevent and treat heart disease and about some of the surgical procedures that have been developed.

You may also want to consider the possibility that one of the many **complementary therapies now available** could help you – especially by encouraging you to relax and feel less stressed.

Chapter 5 contains a rundown of some of those you might find helpful, with details of how they work and how to find a reputable complementary practitioner.

Chapter 6 is devoted to outlining all the exciting discoveries that have been made about **food and diet and how they can help to promote healthier arteries**. It includes advice on what foods to choose and the best cooking methods to use. It also gives details about some of the different nutrients that have been found to help protect against heart disease and improve blood fat levels, as well as some of the different world cuisines that have been found to be beneficial for the heart.

Finally, the book includes a selection of **60 recipes** designed to tempt your taste buds whilst incorporating the latest knowledge about the healthiest diet for your heart and blood vessels.

Overall, the goal of this book is to **increase your knowledge of how you can achieve a healthy heart** – whether you have heart disease yourself, are looking after someone with heart disease or are simply interested in living a healthy lifestyle and preventing possible problems with your heart. The more you understand, the better equipped you will be to take your health into your own hands so as to enjoy your life and stay as fit and well as you can for as long as possible.

chapter 1

Watching a tennis or football player, a marathon runner or a professional mountaineer gives you some idea of the astonishing stamina some human beings possess. A strong heart is able to power the body hour after hour as its owner performs the most amazing feats of endurance. However, even in those of us who are not top sportspeople the heart is an incredible organ. Second by second, every hour of every day from the time you were in the uterus, your heart beats ceaselessly and rhythmically, never pausing for rest. In fact, **the heart works harder than any other muscle in your body**, beating more than 2,500 million times during the course of your lifetime. A strong and efficient heart is one of the secrets of a long and healthy life.

The heart's job is to deliver a continuous **supply of oxygen and nutrients from your blood to your body's cells and tissues** in order for them to perform the myriad tasks they have to do. After oxygen and nutrients have been delivered to the cells, the blood containing unwanted carbon dioxide and other waste materials is carried back to the heart.

If anything impedes this process the heart will not work as efficiently. To understand **what can go wrong in heart disease**, you need to know a bit about how the heart and the blood vessels work.

the heart

THE STRUCTURE OF THE HEART

The heart is a muscular organ about the size of two clenched fists. It consists of a double pump situated in the middle of your chest. The size of the heart and how efficient it is depend on your physical fitness. Athletes and others who exercise a lot or are very active have larger, stronger hearts which are more efficient – that is, they beat more slowly to deliver the same amount of blood as the heart of a less fit person. The good news is that it is possible to build up the efficiency of your heart by cardiovascular exercise, or 'training'.

The walls of the heart are made of a special type of muscle, called the myocardium. Like any other muscle, the myocardium depends on oxygen and nutrients from the bloodstream. But unlike the muscles in your arms and legs, say, which only move when your brain tells them to, the heart contracts automatically without any conscious stimulus.

The right third of your heart lies to the right of your breastbone. The remaining two-thirds are situated to the left of your breastbone, with the rounded point of the heart, known as the apex, tilted slightly forward just below your left nipple. If you feel between your fifth and sixth ribs at this point – known medically as the point of maximal intensity – you should be able to feel your heart beating where the apex touches the chest wall. This is known as the apex beat.

The interior of the heart contains four main chambers: the right atrium (from the Latin word *atrium* meaning entrance hall) and the right ventricle (from another Latin word meaning underside), and the left atrium and left ventricle. The atria are the upper chambers, which receive blood into the heart; the ventricles are the discharging chambers, which pump blood from the heart and out into the circulation. These chambers are in effect muscular bags whose walls contract rhythmically, stimulated by electrical currents to push blood to your lungs and around your body.

The two sides of the heart – that is, the left and right atria and the left and right ventricles – are separated by a thick central wall of muscle known as the septum.

The internal surface of the heart is lined with a smooth protective membrane known as the endocardium, and the whole structure is enclosed in a tough, fibrous bag called the pericardium, which also covers the roots of the major blood vessels.

THE FUNCTION OF THE HEART

The heart's role is to pump blood around two circuits, known as the pulmonary circuit (from the Latin *pulmonus* meaning lung), which serves the lungs, and the systemic circuit, which serves the rest of the body. The right side of the heart serves the lungs – that is, the pulmonary circuit – while the left side of the heart serves the rest of the body – that is, the systemic circuit.

BELOW: Healthy coronary arteries, shown here on an arteriograph (an X-ray photograph of the arteries), are vital for a strong, healthy heart.

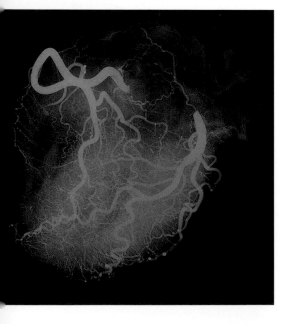

Like any muscular tissue, the thickness of the walls of the heart depends on the amount of work they do. Although equal volumes of blood flow through the heart's two circuits, the pulmonary circuit served by the right ventricle has to work less hard because the journey to the lungs is short and unimpeded. The left ventricle is a much more powerful pump because the systemic circuit wends its way around the whole body. In the process, it encounters about five times as much friction or resistance to blood flow. To accommodate this extra workload, the walls of the left ventricle are two to three times thicker than those of the right ventricle.

The heart valves
As with many other pumps, the blood in the heart is kept flowing in the right direction by a system of valves: the pulmonary and tricuspid valves on the right of the heart, and the aortic and mitral valves on the left of the heart. These four valves open and close automatically to let blood through and prevent it from flowing backwards. With each heartbeat, the atria contract and propel blood into the relaxed ventricles. When the ventricles fill with blood they in turn contract.

The cardiac cycle
The pumping action of the heart has two distinct phases, which together make up a cycle of one heart beat. This is known as the cardiac cycle. The two phases are known as systole and diastole. During diastole (the resting phase), the ventricles relax and the heart fills with blood. Deoxygenated blood flows into the right side of the heart, and oxygenated blood flows into the left side. Towards the end of this phase, an electrical impulse starts and spreads over the atria and to the ventricles. This triggers the second phase, or systole. During this phase, the upper chambers of the heart – the atria – contract, squeezing blood into the ventricles, which then in turn contract, pumping deoxygenated blood into the pulmonary artery and oxygenated blood into the aorta. When the heart is empty, the whole cycle begins again.

You will hear the terms diastole and systole in relation to your blood pressure. When doctors or nurses measure blood pressure, they take two measurements: the systolic blood pressure (the first figure in a blood pressure reading) when the heart is contracted and blood is being pumped out, and the diastolic blood pressure (the second figure) when the heart is relaxed. So, if your blood pressure is 130/80, the systolic pressure is 130 and the diastolic pressure is 80. The pressure in the blood vessels is at its peak during the phase when the heart is contracting.

The whole process depends on a complex system of electrical timing, or conduction. The electrical impulse that causes the heart to pump originates in the cells of the myocardium and travels through a network of special fibres. It is controlled by the sinoatrial node, or sinus node, a tiny bundle of specialized cells found in the right atrium, also known as the

ABOVE: The heart is forced to beat harder and faster when you do any kind of aerobic exercise. Over time this leads to a stronger, more efficient heart.

the heart and blood vessels

heart's pacemaker. Impulses are transmitted through the pacemaker to the atria, causing them to contract.

Another node, called the atrioventricular node, found at the junction of the atria and the ventricles, passes the impulses down through another bundle of fibres, called the bundle of His, to the muscles of the ventricles, causing them to contract in their turn.

Factors influencing the heart's activity

The rate at which your heart beats and the amount of blood it pumps out – the cardiac output – varies with each heartbeat, depending on your muscles' need for oxygen. If you are sitting down or are inactive, your heart will beat about 60 to 80 times a minute and pump out around 80 millilitres (ml) of blood with each stroke – around 6 litres a minute. However, if you are doing an aerobics class, running for a bus or exerting yourself in some other way, your heart rate can rise to a staggering 200 beats a minute and the output of blood can increase to 250ml per beat – as much as 50 litres a minute.

These changes in heart rate and output depend on two factors. In the first place, the heart responds to an increase in blood flowing in by increasing its output. This is because the more the ventricles fill with blood the more strongly they contract to pump out blood during the systolic phase of the cycle. Secondly, the heart is controlled automatically by a cluster of specialized nerve cells in the brain known as the cardiac centre. When you are resting, the cardiac centre transmits messages along a nerve called the vagus nerve, telling the heart to slow down. If you are active or preparing to be active, nerves known as sympathetic nerves come into play. These release a hormone messenger called adrenaline (epinephrine) that causes the heart to beat more quickly and forcefully. The same process happens, even if you are inactive, when you are under stress, anxious or afraid. In this case, the body anticipates action in the form of having to run away or fight (the so-called 'fight or flight' reaction) and releases adrenaline, causing the heart to beat harder.

THE CIRCULATION

The circulation consists of the entire network of blood vessels – arteries, veins and capillaries – that are responsible for maintaining a constant supply of life-giving blood to all the body's tissues and organs.

Structure and function

As we have already seen, the circulatory system has two main parts: the systemic circulation, which serves the whole body except the lungs; and the pulmonary circulation, which carries spent blood to the lungs for reoxygenation.

BELOW: At rest your heart slows down and less blood is pumped out with each stroke – unless, that is, you are watching a scary movie!

The systemic circulation starts at the left side of the heart, where the left atrium receives blood from the lungs. This bright red, oxygen-rich blood passes into the left ventricle, which pumps the blood out into the arteries via the aorta, the body's main artery. The blood is then carried through other smaller arteries, called arterioles, which supply the body's organs. The arterioles branch into a network of even smaller vessels called capillaries. The capillary walls are extremely thin (one cell thick), and this allows oxygen and nutrients to pass from the blood into the tissues, and carbon dioxide and other waste products to pass into the blood in exchange. Most of the waste is dropped off as the blood passes through the kidneys, and is processed into urine.

The capillaries, now transporting deoxygenated blood, deliver the blood into small veins known as venules. These join to form larger veins which carry the dark, oxygen-depleted blood (a purplish-red rather than blue) into the venae cava, the body's main veins. These then carry the blood to the right atrium from where it passes into the right ventricle. From here it is pumped to the lungs via the pulmonary circulation, where it unloads waste carbon dioxide and picks up a fresh supply of oxygen, derived from the air breathed in, which it then delivers to the left atrium ... and so the cycle continues.

Intriguingly, in the pulmonary circulation the jobs of the arteries and veins are reversed. The blood in the arteries is oxygen-depleted (as it carries blood to the lungs). Meanwhile, the blood in the veins is oxygen-rich as it carries refreshed blood back to the heart.

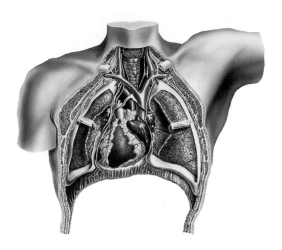

ABOVE: The body's main vein, the venae cava, shown here in blue, delivers deoxygenated blood to the heart from the body. The main artery, the aorta, shown in red, pumps oxygenated blood from the lungs to the body.

THE HEART'S BLOOD SUPPLY

Like any other muscle, the heart needs oxygen to work efficiently. But although the heart is constantly pumping blood to other parts of the body, it does not obtain much oxygen from this blood. To obtain its own supply of oxygen the heart muscle depends on the two coronary arteries which arise from the aorta. These arteries supply the whole heart with oxygen.

WHAT CAN GO WRONG?

There are a huge number of disorders that can affect the cardiovascular system. They range from congenital heart defects present at birth to high blood pressure, heart failure, arrhythmias (disorders of the heart rhythm), valvular heart disease and various diseases affecting the heart muscle (cardiomyopathies) which affect the functioning of the heart. However, when people talk about heart disease, or coronary heart disease to use the full medical term, what they usually mean is a combination of different symptoms caused by the narrowing (atherosclerosis) of the coronary arteries serving the heart. It is this type of heart disease that is the subject of this book.

The term heart disease is actually rather misleading because it suggests that it is the heart itself which is diseased. In fact, heart disease – or coronary heart disease (CHD) to use the correct medical term – more accurately refers to the narrowing of the arteries that makes the heart work less effectively and produces **symptoms such as angina (chest pain) and heart attack**.

As we saw in Chapter 1, the heart is a muscle that depends on oxygen and nutrients to do its job of pumping blood around the body and to and from the lungs. These are carried to the heart in the two coronary arteries. If something happens to impede the flow of blood through these arteries, **the heart is unable to do its job efficiently**.

The blood flow can be impeded in two ways: firstly, by **a build-up of a substance called atheroma in the lining of the artery walls**; and, secondly, by **a thrombosis, or blood clot, blocking one of the arteries supplying the heart**. Both of these are closely related to various changes that take place in the arteries over a period of many years.

atherosclerosis

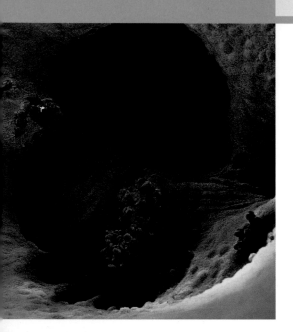

ABOVE: One of the main causes of a heart attack is blockage of a coronary artery by a blood clot, or thrombosis, seen here at the entrance to one of the coronary arteries.

The overwhelming cause of angina and virtually all heart attacks is athero-sclerosis, otherwise known as hardening and narrowing of the arteries. The term comes from two Greek words, *atheroma* meaning porridge and *scleros* meaning hard. It happens when the inner lining of the artery walls becomes furred with a thick, porridge-like sludge called atheroma.

Over time, the arteries may become so narrow that they are unable to deliver oxygen-carrying blood to the heart and other parts of the body, leading to ischaemia, or lack of blood. People with hardened and narrowed arteries are also more prone to blood clotting, partly because blood flow is more sluggish and partly because of complicated physical and chemical changes in the artery walls and the blood that make the blood more likely to clot.

Atherosclerosis is a complicated process involving many different stages. In fact, it usually takes 20 years or more to develop to the point where it becomes troublesome.

The exact reasons why atherosclerosis builds up are still being invest-igated. However, experts agree that many different factors can increase the risk or likelihood of it developing. One of the main players is cholesterol.

plaque formation

Atheroma is made up of fatty deposits of LDLs ('bad cholesterol') together with other debris such as cell waste, calcium (a mineral) and fibrin (the substance that forms clots in the blood). These mix together to form raised patches on the artery wall known as plaques. These narrow the arteries so that the space the blood has to flow through is reduced, a bit like a river getting silted up.

THE CHOLESTEROL STORY

There was a time when cholesterol seemed straightforward: high levels bad, low levels good. However, as doctors have learnt more about the process of atherosclerosis a more complicated picture has emerged.

Cholesterol is a waxy, fatty substance made in the body mainly by the liver but also in the intestines and other cells. Contrary to popular opinion, cholesterol in itself is not bad. It is needed by your body to produce hor-mones, including sex hormones such as oestrogen and progesterone. It also helps the liver to produce bile salts, which are needed to digest fat. It is involved in the synthesis of vitamin D and it is also the main ingredient of cell membranes – for example, it helps to form the myelin sheath, the protective coating that covers the nerves.

By the basic laws of chemistry, oil and water do not mix. This means that cholesterol, being a fatty substance, cannot travel alone in the blood, which consists mainly of water. Instead, it is transported in special carrier proteins called lipoproteins, and this is where the picture becomes slightly more complicated because there are two main kinds of lipoproteins.

The first are LDLs – low-density lipoproteins – popularly known as 'bad cholesterol' because of their role in depositing cholesterol in the arteries. The second are HDLs – high-density lipoproteins – also known as 'good cholesterol' because they help to sweep cholesterol away from the artery walls. Put simply, LDLs transport cholesterol to the body's cells from the liver while HDLs clear excess cholesterol from the arteries and carry it back to the liver, thus helping to protect against heart disease. So, to avoid heart disease, you need high levels of HDLs and low levels of LDLs.

HOW ATHEROSCLEROSIS DEVELOPS

The first step in the development of atherosclerosis occurs when LDL cholesterol becomes oxidized. Oxidation is a chemical reaction which causes metal to rust, a cut apple to turn brown and butter to go rancid. In the body, oxidation is caused by free radicals, harmful molecules produced as a result of damage to cells by blood-borne chemicals such as nicotine, high levels of blood glucose, viruses, pollution or physical factors such as injury or high blood pressure.

In heart disease, it is the smooth muscle cells lining the arteries, known as endothelial cells, that are affected. If these become damaged, a complex chemical reaction is set in motion in which LDLs become oxidized, damaging neighbouring cells and unleashing a cascade of chemicals which in turn trigger the release of blood cells produced by the body's immune system. These travel to the damaged or injured area in order to try to heal the injury to the epithelium.

Unfortunately, some of these cells become laden down with fats and become what are known as 'foam cells'. They are then joined by smooth muscle cells, which also absorb fat and in turn become foam cells. As foam cells accumulate over time they form 'fatty streaks' in the arteries. As time goes on, other debris accumulates in the area to form fatty, fibrous mounds on the walls of the arteries. These are called plaques.

The clotting factor

In normal circumstances, the endothelial cells release chemical agents designed to make the blood vessels widen, or vasodilate, to allow more blood to flow through and to prevent small blood cells called platelets from clumping together to form clots, a process called platelet aggregation. The presence of oxidized LDLs interferes with the release of these chemical agents. This is thought to be a reason why people with atherosclerosis are more prone to blood clotting than other people.

the triglyceride connection

Triglycerides, another fatty ingredient produced by the liver and found in the bloodstream, also play a role in heart disease, especially in women and people with diabetes. Triglyceride levels rise after a fatty meal, like fried fish and chips, say, but are generally low when you are fasting. There is a great deal of debate about the precise role of triglycerides in heart disease, and the connection is not as clear cut as between cholesterol and heart disease. However, what has been found is that, if you have high levels of both LDLs and triglycerides, and especially if these are combined with low levels of HDLs, you have a higher risk of heart disease. Because triglycerides are fatty, like cholesterol, they are carried in the bloodstream in protein molecules, in this case very-low-density lipoproteins, or VLDLs. At first VLDLs carry both triglycerides and cholesterol; however, once they have dropped off their triglyceride load VLDLs become LDLs. Doctors describe VLDLs as precursors of LDLs.

The final stage

The last stage in the development of heart disease is known as arteriosclerosis. This happens when the growing plaques interfere with the delivery of nutrients to the deep tissues of the arterial walls. As a result, smooth muscle cells die and the walls lose their elasticity. Non-elastic scar tissue forms and calcium salts are dumped in the plaques, which cause the walls of the arteries to fray or ulcerate. The growing rigidity of the artery walls leads to high blood pressure, increasing the risk of heart attack.

ISCHAEMIA

Eventually the arteries become so narrow and hardened that blood has great difficulty reaching the heart, which then becomes starved of nutrients and oxygen. This is known as ischaemia, the main sign of which is angina – in other words, chest pain. If the arteries become so narrow that blood is unable to reach the heart, or if a clot forms and blocks the narrowed arteries, a heart attack occurs.

WHICH ARTERIES ARE AFFECTED?

Atherosclerosis can occur in any or all of the arteries, but it is most serious in the coronary arteries that serve the heart. Other arteries commonly affected are those in the legs and arms, the carotid artery serving the brain, the arteries serving the abdomen, and the iliac arteries serving the pelvis. Depending on which arteries are affected, various symptoms may be experienced.

BELOW: Magnetic resonance imaging (MRI) scanning may be used to view the heart and arteries in the diagnosis of heart disease.

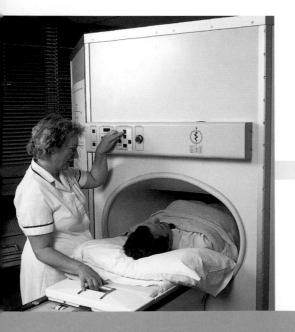

symptoms of coronary artery disease

When atherosclerosis affects the coronary arteries surrounding the heart, angina and/or heart attacks may occur.

ANGINA

If you have coronary artery disease, the heart usually ticks over without too much trouble when you are at rest. However, when you exert yourself in any way the heart's need for oxygen increases and there is an imbalance between supply and demand, causing angina, or angina pectoris as it is known medically (literally 'choked chest').

Angina is the most important clue that your arteries have become narrowed and hardened. Although it is not in itself fatal, it is important to take it seriously as it is a sign that your heart is not receiving enough oxygen.

Angina is variously described as a feeling of pressure, heaviness, discomfort or pain in the centre of the chest, that may spread to the arms, neck, shoulder, jaw, face or stomach. The pain usually begins gradually and lasts for up to ten minutes, before ebbing away if you stop whatever it is that is triggering it or take medication.

Angina is the result of the heart muscle receiving insufficient oxygen and nutrients from the narrowed arteries. As the tissues of the heart become starved of oxygen, or ischaemic, they produce chemicals which irritate nerve fibres in the heart, sending pain messages from the chest to the brain.

Triggers of angina

Angina is most often triggered by exercise or exertion – for example, running for a bus, playing tennis, climbing stairs or walking up a hill. It can also be triggered by other factors. For example, many people experience angina more often in cold weather. This is because when it is cold the blood vessels constrict, increasing the amount of work the heart has to do as well as reducing the amount of blood that gets to the heart. Angina may also come on after a heavy meal because when you are digesting food, blood pools in the stomach and intestines, thus increasing the work of the heart. Stress is another trigger, again because the blood vessels constrict when you are anxious or stressed as a result of the release of adrenaline (epinephrine), the stress hormone, as part of the body's 'fight or flight' reaction.

Types of angina

There are two types of angina: stable angina and unstable angina. In stable angina, pain is experienced after a particular amount of exertion. This is why people with angina can often predict that they are going to experience it after, say, ten minutes' walking or on climbing the stairs.

Sometimes, however, the pain of angina comes and goes unpredictably. For example, it comes on after less exertion or while you are sitting. This is known as unstable angina. Because unstable angina often precedes a heart attack, it is important to report any change of pattern to your doctor.

SILENT ISCHAEMIA

Although angina is unpleasant, in some ways people who suffer it are lucky because the pain usually makes them stop what they are doing. A small proportion of people with coronary artery disease experience no

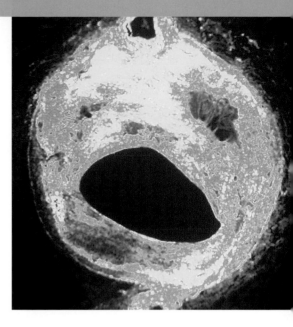

ABOVE: A cross-section of arterial walls showing furring of the artery with atherosclerosis. Note how the amount of space left for blood to flow through is narrowed.

ABOVE: The earlier a heart attack is diagnosed and treated, the better the chances of recovery.

symptoms when the heart is short of oxygen. This is known as silent ischaemia. People with diabetes are more prone to silent ischaemia, because diabetes may damage the nerve fibres so that pain is not experienced. The problem with this is that, without the warning of pain, they are unaware that the heart is short of blood and are less likely to stop doing whatever it is that has triggered the ischaemia.

HEART ATTACK (MYOCARDIAL INFARCTION)

If one of the coronary arteries becomes completely blocked, either by atherosclerosis or by a blood clot (a thrombosis), the heart muscle is totally deprived of oxygen and nutrients and this causes the heart muscle cells to die and be replaced by scar tissue. This is a heart attack, or myocardial infarction (literally 'death of the heart') to use the correct medical term.

In the past, doctors thought that it was lack of oxygen in itself that caused the heart muscle cells to die. However, it is now known that problems actually occur when blood starts to flow back to the area previously deprived of blood, a process known as reperfusion.

When the blood begins to flow back to the heart following a heart attack, lymphocytes (white blood cells) and other inflammatory cells gather in the area in an attempt to repair the damage. These start a chemical cascade that results in a flood of free radicals (harmful molecules that damage cells, see page 66) and the release of the chemical nitric oxide, which is involved in opening up the blood vessels. These depress the heart's ability to contract properly and at the same time damage the heart tissue.

atherosclerosis in other arteries

TRANSIENT ISCHAEMIC ATTACK (TIA) AND STROKE

Atherosclerosis can also occur in the carotid artery, the main blood vessel supplying the brain. In this case, it may cause transient ischaemic attacks (TIAs), or mini-strokes – brief periods when the brain is deprived of its blood supply – or, if the blood is totally unable to reach the brain, a full-blown stroke. A TIA is a sign that the brain is not getting enough blood, in much the same way as angina is a sign that the heart is not getting enough blood. A stroke is a sign that the brain has been completely deprived of blood, either because the arteries have become so narrowed that blood cannot get through or because the arteries have been blocked by a clot. In fact, a stroke is to the brain what a heart attack is to the heart. This is why a stroke is sometimes known as a brain attack. People who have heart attacks are at an increased risk of stroke and TIAs, and vice versa.

PERIPHERAL VASCULAR DISEASE

Atherosclerosis may also affect the blood supply to the legs, causing peripheral vascular disease, or PVD. In PVD, the blood vessels supplying the legs become ever narrower as a result of atherosclerosis, causing a condition known as intermittent claudication – pain in the calves or thighs after walking or exercising the legs. This is a sign that the leg muscles are not getting enough nutrients and oxygen, just as angina is a sign that the heart muscle is not getting enough nutrients and oxygen. Other clues are cold or painful toes, redness or a bluish discolouration.

OTHER HEART PROBLEMS

ATRIAL FIBRILLATION
A type of rapid heart beat, in which the upper chambers of the heart (the atria) beat quickly and irregularly so blood is not pumped efficiently to the ventricles, causing palpitations, weakness, light-headedness, nausea, shortness of breath or occasionally fainting. It is more common in people with atherosclerosis or high blood pressure.

FAMILIAL HYPERCHOLESTEROLAEMIA OR HYPER-LIPIDAEMIA
Inheritance of higher than normal levels of cholesterol, causing an increased risk of atherosclerosis and heart disease.

ENDOCARDITIS
Infection of the lining of the heart and heart valves most common in people whose hearts have been damaged by rheumatic fever or are abnormal due to a congenital or degenerative disorder. Intra-venous drug users who inject using dirty needles are also at risk.

VALVULAR HEART DISEASE
Disease or damage to one or more of the four valves in the heart caused by congenital heart disease, rheumatic fever or ageing. In valve stenosis, the valve does not open fully, obstructing the flow of blood so the heart has to pump more powerfully to force blood past the obstruction. In valve incompetence or regurgitation, the valve does not close properly so that blood leaks backwards. This means the heart has to work harder to pump the necessary volume of blood forwards, and back pressure caused by blood behind the affected valve occurs. This in turn can cause fluid to accumulate in the lungs or lower body.

CARDIOMYOPATHY
This term encompasses several diseases affecting the heart muscles. They can cause thickening of the muscle around the valve, leading to obstruction of the valve.

CONGESTIVE HEART FAILURE
When the heart pumps inefficiently as a result of damage to the heart muscles caused by atherosclerosis, heart attack, valvular heart disease or other causes to do with the lungs. Blood returning from the veins then backs up in other tissues, rather like water building up behind a dam. This can cause fluid to accumulate in the lungs.

CARDIAC ARRHYTHMIAS
Disturbances of the heart rhythm caused by abnormalities in the signalling mechanism that controls the heart beat. One of the most common arrhythmias is atrial fibrillation (see left). It is linked to high blood pressure, stroke, coronary heart disease, valvular disease and an overactive thyroid.

HEART BLOCK
When the electrical impulses of the heart are slowed or delayed, causing the heart rate or rhythm to be affected. There are varying degrees of heart block. However, in complete heart block electrical messages do not cross to the ventricles, and the atria and ventricles beat independently. It can be caused by atherosclerosis and ageing, or may happen after a heart operation. It can also affect people with an enlarged heart caused by untreated high blood pressure or rheumatic heart disease.

ABOVE: Angina pectoris – commonly known simply as angina – is a sign that not enough oxygen is reaching the heart. It is particularly a symptom of heart disease in men.

who is at risk of heart disease?

Although the precise causes of heart disease are still not fully understood, certain factors can increase your likelihood of developing it. These are known as risk factors.

There are two kinds of risk factors: ones you cannot do anything about (such as your age, gender or ethnic group) and others which you can modify (such as your eating habits, smoking and the amount of exercise you do).

To understand more about how heart disease may affect you personally, you need to work out your personal risk rating. By and large the more risk factors you have the greater your odds of developing heart disease. Many risk factors are linked to other risk factors. For example, diabetes is linked both to high blood pressure and to high levels of blood fats and obesity.

Having said this, an important thing to bear in mind about risk factors is that they are not set in stone. Risk factors are worked out by studying patterns of disease in large groups of people, a scientific body of knowledge known as epidemiology. However, epidemiology is not an exact science precisely because it does deal with large groups and does not say anything about you as an individual. So, having one or more risk factors does not mean that you are doomed to develop heart disease any more than not having them offers a guarantee that you will never have a heart attack.

Furthermore, once you know what risk factors apply to you, it is possible to take steps to protect yourself and so lower your risk. In the past, the relevance of risk factors was mainly to people avoiding risk. However, in recent years scientists have made many exciting discoveries, especially about food and the role it can play in actively protecting against heart disease. In the next chapter and in Chapter 6, you will discover a whole host of achievable measures that you can take to reduce or modify your risk factors, including foods that can actively help to protect your blood vessels.

YOUR AGE

Most heart attacks happen in men aged over 45 and women aged over 55, so your risk of having a heart attack will increase as you get older.

As we have seen, atherosclerosis takes a long time to develop and people are usually middle-aged or older by the time it is sufficiently advanced to produce symptoms. Meanwhile, the arteries naturally become less elastic as we age as a result of the degenerative changes of ageing, leading to a greater risk of high blood pressure, which is a separate risk factor for heart disease.

Although you cannot, of course, turn back the clock, by eating a healthy diet and taking other steps to live a healthier life you may be able to slow or delay age-related changes in the arteries.

YOUR GENDER

Men are more likely to develop atherosclerosis than women, at least until middle age. This is because the female sex hormone oestrogen actively protects against heart disease by creating a more favourable balance of blood fats and by contributing to the elasticity and health of the arteries. However, after the menopause – or following a total hysterectomy in which the ovaries are removed as well as the uterus, thus depriving the body of oestrogen – this natural protection vanishes and women's risk of developing heart disease rises to equal that of men, especially in women smokers.

Taking HRT – hormone replacement therapy – the main ingredient of which is oestrogen, has been found in many studies to help protect women against heart disease after the menopause.

YOUR GENES

If there is a history of heart disease or factors predisposing to heart disease in your family, such as high cholesterol levels (see familial hypercholesterolaemia page 21) or high blood pressure, you are more at risk of developing it yourself.

To estimate your risk you could draw up a family tree on which you note those members who developed heart disease. The more first-degree relatives – that is, mother, father, brother or sister – with heart disease, especially those who developed it at a young age (before age 55 for your father or brother or before 65 for your mother or sister), the greater your risk.

The publication of the human genome – the 'book of life' containing the entire set of genes that go to make up a human being – in June 2000 marked a milestone in the understanding of the genetic basis of diseases. Scientists are now working hard to try and pinpoint exactly which genes may be involved in various diseases, including heart disease, with the aim of finding ways in which they may be modified by drug treatment or eventually by gene therapy to correct faulty genes.

Some genes can affect the way in which cholesterol and fat behave in the blood, and so predispose to heart attacks. It is these genes that are involved in the condition known as familial hypercholesterolaemia.

There is still a great deal to learn about the genes involved in heart disease, but in time it is likely that scientists will identify many more genes

BELOW: An electrocardiogram (ECG) stress test is commonly used to see how the heart responds to exercise.

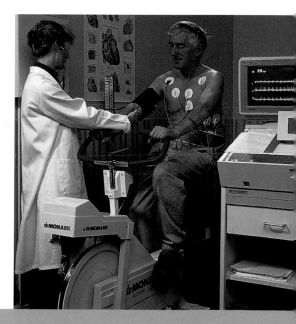

that may play a part. Having said this, however, it is important to bear in mind that your genes are not your destiny. Heart disease is a multifactorial disease, which means that many different factors from your genes, which are not under your control, and from your environment, many aspects of which are under your control, play a part. By modifying environmental factors and taking any drugs the doctor may prescribe it is possible to lower your risk, even if your genes predispose you to heart disease.

In addition, unhealthy habits, like smoking, taking little or no exercise and dietary preferences, are often learnt in the family. So, if your parents smoke you are more likely to take up the habit yourself. Likewise, if you learnt to enjoy fatty foods as a child because those foods were on the family menu you may have developed a preference for those foods, although it is always possible to adopt healthier eating habits. These are things that it is possible to do something about and thus cut your risk of heart disease.

YOUR ETHNIC BACKGROUND

In the UK, people of south Asian origin are more at risk of heart disease. This is partly because south Asians have a higher risk of developing diabetes, which is itself a risk factor for heart disease. Diabetes, in turn, is linked to a phenomenon known as insulin resistance, in which the body produces insulin but is unable to use it properly, with the result that high levels of blood glucose develop in the bloodstream.

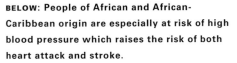

BELOW: People of African and African-Caribbean origin are especially at risk of high blood pressure which raises the risk of both heart attack and stroke.

People of African and African-Caribbean origin in the UK and African-Americans in the USA are also at increased risk of heart disease (but particularly of stroke), although there is a different cause-and-effect mechanism at work. People of African origin are more likely to develop high blood pressure, a risk factor for both heart disease and stroke. Although the reasons for this are unknown and are likely to include both genetic and environmental factors, it is thought to be at least partly a result of a fault in a gene that enables the body to handle salt.

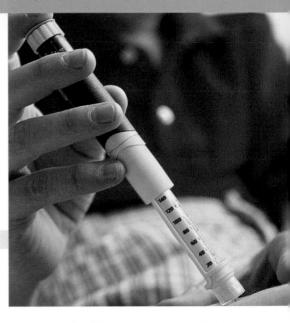

ABOVE: People with diabetes are at a higher risk of developing cardiovascular disease although the exact mechanisms that raise the risk have yet to be fully unravelled.

DIABETES

Diabetes increases your risk of heart disease two- or threefold if you are a man and four- to fivefold if you are a premenopausal woman. Heart attacks are two to three times more common in people with diabetes, and the risk of heart failure is five times more. If you have diabetes, you are also at an increased risk of intermittent claudication caused by narrowed arteries in the legs. People with diabetes are more likely to have silent ischaemia detected by electrocardiogram (ECG) monitoring.

The risk of developing cardiovascular disease is especially high among people who develop type 2 diabetes, which most often strikes in middle age. Obesity and inactivity – both separate risk factors for heart disease – both increase your risk of developing type 2 diabetes. Unfortunately, because in the early stages diabetes may produce no symptoms, many people with the condition remain undiagnosed, sometimes for many years, during which time their arteries may be becoming ever more damaged.

Diabetes is a result of a fault in the mechanism whereby glucose in the blood is converted into energy. This process is governed by the hormone insulin, which is produced by the pancreas after eating. In diabetes, either the pancreas fails to produce sufficient insulin or the insulin it produces is unable to be used, which is known as insulin resistance. Insulin resistance is more common in people who are overweight and who carry their excess weight around the middle – that is, who are 'apple' as opposed to 'pear' shaped. This pattern of fat distribution is linked to a higher risk of heart disease, even when the person does not develop fully fledged diabetes.

Doctors do not fully understand the mechanism by which diabetes increases the risk of heart disease. However, what is known is that people with the non-insulin-dependent form of diabetes – that is, who have their diabetes controlled by drugs and/or medication but do not have to inject insulin – tend to have low levels of protective HDL cholesterol and higher levels of damaging LDL cholesterol, and they also tend to have a higher level of triglycerides, especially after fatty meals. High blood pressure, an

ABOVE: Drinking heavily or binge drinking can raise blood pressure and increase the risk of heart disease.

independent risk factor for heart disease, is also more common in people with diabetes, probably due to raised insulin levels.

Of course, the major risk factors for heart disease among people without diabetes – such as high blood pressure, raised cholesterol levels, smoking, obesity and physical inactivity – still apply if you have diabetes. However, the extra risk of heart disease is only partly explained by higher levels of these other risk factors. Diabetes appears to be a separate extra risk and may possibly amplify the risk of these other factors.

HIGH BLOOD PRESSURE (HYPERTENSION)

Tremendous force is needed to pump blood out of your heart and around your body. Blood pressure is the force of blood in your arteries. The pressure of blood travelling in the arteries is determined by how hard your heart works and the health of your blood vessels, and varies quite normally throughout the day. For example, it rises temporarily during the day, with exercise or exertion, in cold weather, if you smoke a cigarette or if you are excited or angry. It is lower at night, when you are relaxed, when you are asleep or when you are listening to quiet music.

High blood pressure (or hypertension) – that is, when the pressure is persistently higher than it should be – increases your risk of heart disease, stroke and other problems such as congestive heart failure, peripheral vascular disease and kidney problems.

Blood pressure is measured when the heart is at rest and when it is contracting (see Chapter 1), and the two figures are recorded. Blood pressure is naturally higher when the heart is contracting – systolic pressure, the first figure in a blood pressure reading – and lower between beats when the heart is at rest – diastolic pressure, the second figure in a blood pressure reading. Blood pressure is measured in units called millimetres of mercury (mmHg). An average blood pressure in a healthy, young person is around 120/80mmHg. There is no set level at which high blood pressure is diagnosed. However, doctors often define hypertension as a blood pressure of above 140/85mmHg, or 140/80mmHg if you have diabetes.

When blood pressure is persistently high, the strain on the arteries is enormous. As a result, the smooth lining of the arteries becomes rough and the walls become thicker, which in turn causes the arteries to narrow and become less elastic.

The insidious thing about high blood pressure is that it usually produces no symptoms, but it can still be damaging your blood vessels. This is why it is important to have your blood pressure checked regularly, so that if it is raised you can take steps to reduce it.

risk factors for high blood pressure

You are more at risk of high blood pressure if:

→ you have a family history of the condition.
→ you are overweight.
→ you drink heavily or to excess.
→ you eat a very salty diet.
→ you are under stress.
→ you have narrowed arteries because of kidney disease.
→ you are a black African, African-Caribbean or African-American.

HIGH LEVELS OF BLOOD FATS

Higher than normal levels of blood fats or lipids (cholesterol and triglycerides, see pages 16 and 17) are an important risk factor for heart disease, as we have seen. Factors predisposing towards high blood fat levels include eating a diet high in saturated fats, being overweight and lack of exercise.

Blood fats are measured in units known as millimoles per litre (mmol/l). The average blood cholesterol level of people in the UK is 5.8mmol/l. In China the average reading is just 3.2mmol/l. Like blood pressure levels, lipid levels can vary tremendously from one day to another and at different times of the day. A single high reading may be of no significance. However, if you have persistently raised levels of blood cholesterol, especially if your LDL levels are high and your HDL levels are low, it is worthwhile taking steps to reduce them.

causes of high blood cholesterol levels:

→ **eating a fatty diet, especially one that is high in saturated animal fats.**
→ **underactive thyroid gland.**
→ **chronic renal (kidney) failure.**
→ **heavy drinking or alcohol abuse.**
→ **the inherited condition familial hyperlipidaemia.**

SMOKING

Smoking increases your risk of having a heart attack two- or threefold. In fact, smokers aged under 50 are a staggering 5 times more likely to die of heart disease than people who do not smoke. Smoking is also the premier risk factor for sudden cardiac death (having an unexpected fatal heart attack) and peripheral vascular disease.

Smoking affects the health of your heart and blood vessels in several ways. Firstly, nicotine triggers the release of the stress hormone adrenaline

BELOW: Smoking greatly increases the risk of dying of heart disease.

the fibrinogen factor

Fibrinogen is an ingredient in your blood – a protein that causes it to become thicker and more viscose by making platelets, the blood cells involved in clotting, stickier. Studies have suggested that raised fibrinogen levels are a risk factor for heart attack and stroke, although scientists do not yet fully understand why this may be. One clue has come from research which has found that a variation in a gene that codes for fibrinogen is triggered by smoking. The researchers suggested that raised levels of fibrinogen caused by the faulty gene could lead to excessive clotting and inflammation, leading to a greater risk of heart attack and/or stroke.

High fibrinogen levels have also been found to be a potential warning sign of the presence of a particularly dangerous form of LDL, or 'bad cholesterol', in the bloodstream. Women have naturally higher levels of fibrinogen, which could be one reason why smoking is particularly dangerous for women. This is an example of how risk factors often work hand in hand to increase the risk of heart disease.

(epinephrine) from the adrenal glands. This increases the heart rate and raises blood pressure, creating a greater need for oxygen in the heart. Secondly, the gas carbon monoxide, found in tobacco smoke, displaces oxygen from the bloodstream, depriving the heart of the oxygen it needs to function efficiently. It is estimated that heavy smokers may be short of as much as 15 per cent of their hearts' oxygen needs. Finally, other chemicals in tobacco and smoke accelerate the narrowing of the arteries by triggering the release of free radicals, the harmful molecules which are an important part of the process by which atherosclerosis develops (see page 17).

OVERWEIGHT

Being overweight increases your risk of heart disease. No one knows exactly why this should be, but one reason is undoubtedly that if you are overweight you are more likely to develop diabetes, which as we have already seen is linked to heart disease. If you are overweight, you are also more likely to have raised blood cholesterol levels and high blood pressure, because excess weight increases the amount of work your heart has to do. Overweight also tends to make it more difficult to be physically active, which can help to protect against heart disease. In fact, even being moderately overweight increases your risk of heart disease by 80 per cent.

If you are overweight, the way fat is distributed is the most important factor in whether or not you are at risk of heart disease. There are two main sites where fat is stored.

In 'apple' shaped people excess fat is stored around the abdomen, producing the classic 'beer belly'. This pattern of fat distribution is more likely to affect men and women after the menopause, as 'middle-aged spread'.

In 'pear' shaped people, mainly among premenopausal women, fat is stored around the hips and buttocks. This pattern of fat distribution, the typical 'hour-glass figure', is healthier for the heart.

In practice, what this means is that, if you are a man, your waist measurement should be no more than 90 per cent of your hip measurement. That means that if your hips are 102cm (40in), your waist should be no more than 91cm (36in)). If you are a woman, your waist should be no more than 80 per cent of your hip measurement. So if your hips are 102cm (40in), ideally your waist should be no more than 81cm (32in).

Apple shaped people are more at risk not only of heart disease but also of high blood pressure, raised blood fat levels, raised blood glucose levels and diabetes. In all these conditions there are high levels of insulin in the blood as a result of insulin resistance (see pages 24–5). In insulin resistance, remember, insulin is produced but cannot be utilized properly by the body. The tendency to a particular shape and insulin resistance is very largely inherited, so if one or both your parents are 'apples', it is worth taking particular care over diet and exercise to lose excess fat and keep your weight in check.

INACTIVITY

Inactivity – watching too much television, taking the car instead of walking, sitting down a lot – can damage the health of your heart. When you are inactive your circulation is reduced, with the result that less oxygen and nutrients are delivered to your body's cells. Lack of activity also decreases your body's ability to extract oxygen from your blood, weakens your bones (leading to a risk of osteoporosis) and your muscles, and encourages high levels of blood fats.

RAISED HOMOCYSTEINE LEVELS

Everyone has heard of cholesterol and recognizes that it plays a part in heart disease. However, not so many people have heard of homocysteine. Yet it is now being hailed as a 'missing link' in the story of heart disease.

Homocysteine is an amino acid – one of the building blocks that make up protein which our bodies use to build tissues. It is derived from another amino acid, called methionine, which is found in foods containing animal protein, such as meat, milk and eggs. Over the past few years it has become evident that high homocysteine levels increase your risk of heart disease. In fact, a high homocysteine level is found in up to one in five people with heart disease.

It is still not understood exactly how raised homocysteine levels damage the arteries. However, in the test tube, high homocysteine levels have been found to damage the endothelium, the lining of the arteries, which as we have already seen is a crucial step in the development of atherosclerosis. High homocysteine levels have also been found to be a key factor in causing cholesterol to oxidize and be transformed into harmful LDL, and also appear to increase blood clotting.

Intriguingly, homocysteine could help to explain how other risk factors for heart disease may exert their damage. For instance, both smoking and inactivity lead to raised homocysteine levels. Meanwhile, before the menopause, women's homocysteine levels are around a fifth lower than those of men, which could help to explain why women are at lower risk of heart disease during their reproductive years. A healthy homocysteine level is considered to be 12mmol/l or less.

ABOVE: The seeds of heart disease are sown in childhood. Overweight, being inactive and eating fatty, processed foods all raise the risk of heart disease.

causes of high homocysteine levels:

→ **insufficient folic acid in the diet.**
→ **insufficient vitamins B6 and B12 in the diet.**
→ **age.**
→ **hypothyroidism (low levels of thyroid hormones).**
→ **kidney disease.**
→ **psoriasis.**
→ **Systemic lupus erythematosus (SLE).**
→ **some drugs such as methotrexate (used to treat rheumatoid arthritis and psoriasis), theophylline (used to treat asthma and bronchitis) and nicotinic acid (used to lower lipid levels).**
→ **homocystinuria, an inherited shortage of enzymes which process homocysteine in the body.**

The previous chapter described all the various risk factors that can increase your likelihood of developing heart problems. The good news is that, by recognizing your personal risk factors and taking steps to alter your lifestyle, **you can do much to moderate many of these factors and have a healthy heart**.

This chapter covers all the things you can do to help **protect your heart and keep your cardiovascular system healthy** – whether or not you already have heart disease.

Most of the measures advised have an effect on several different risk factors. So, for example, by becoming more active you will help to reduce your blood pressure, improve your blood fat profile and control your weight, all of which can **substantially lower your risk of heart disease**.

As effort is its own reward, you will find that once you begin to live a more healthy lifestyle you will **feel so much more fit and well** that you will want to carry on.

helping yourself

the importance of exercise

Being active is absolutely essential to a healthy heart. Remember that your heart is a muscle. Like any other muscle it can be trained to become strong so that it is able to pump more blood with each beat, giving you more stamina, or endurance. But the health of your heart is about more than how hard it pumps. It also involves other more subtle factors, such as how effectively your muscles and tissues absorb oxygen from your blood, your body's ability to maintain healthy levels of blood fats, including cholesterol and triglycerides, and the level of your blood pressure. Exercise is also a great way to help you relax and to control stress levels, which is another risk factor for heart disease. At the same time, once you begin to exercise regularly and feel the benefits, you may be encouraged to live a healthier life generally by eating a healthier diet and giving up harmful habits like smoking.

PLANNING YOUR EXERCISE PROGRAMME

There is no need to join an expensive gym or take part in organized sport unless you want to and will therefore keep it up. Simple activities like walking, gardening, cycling and incorporating more activity into your daily life can be just as effective as a more structured exercise programme.

The key thing to bear in mind is that the exercise you choose should be both enjoyable and safe, especially if you have already been diagnosed with atherosclerosis or if you have had a heart attack.

If you have not exercised for some time, there are several factors to take into account when you are planning an exercise programme. These include your age, whether you are overweight and whether you have any symptoms of heart disease, such as angina, or factors linked to your condition, such as fatigue, as well as your existing level of fitness.

If you do decide to join a gym, the instructors should be made aware if you have high blood pressure and/or any symptoms of heart disease so that a programme can be devised that is both safe and healthy.

Of course, if you have the money, one possible solution is to have your own personal trainer, who can devise a programme tailored to your individual needs. Most of us do not have that luxury, and it is possible to devise your own programme with a bit of research and knowledge.

CHOOSING TYPES OF EXERCISE

There are three main types of exercise which are necessary to help you become fitter and healthier. These are aerobic, strength and muscular endurance, and flexibility, commonly summed up as the three Ss: stamina, strength and suppleness. Although aerobic exercise often receives the most attention, especially in relation to heart disease, it is important not to overlook the other types of exercise for overall fitness.

how much is enough?

If you experience any or all of the following, you may be exercising too intensively:

→ **chest pain (see angina, page 18).**
→ **dizziness, light-headedness or confusion.**
→ **nausea or vomiting.**
→ **cramp-like pains in the legs (see intermittent claudication, page 21).**
→ **pale or bluish skin tone.**
→ **breathlessness lasting for more than ten minutes.**
→ **palpitations (rapid or irregular heart beat).**
→ **continued fatigue (lasting for 24 hours or more).**
→ **insomnia.**
→ **fluid retention (swollen ankles, sudden weight gain).**

Stamina

Aerobic exercise, also known as endurance or cardiovascular exercise, is designed to increase the strength of your heart muscle and thus your stamina. Over a period of time, regular aerobic exercise improves your body's ability to extract oxygen from the blood and transport it to the rest of the body, including your lungs. It also improves the ability of your body to use oxygen efficiently and to burn (or metabolize) fats and carbohydrates for energy. As time goes on, your heart is able to pump more blood with each stroke and so is able to do more for less effort. This is called the training effect. The training effect is the reason why sportspeople, athletes and others who perform regular activity have a slower pulse rate and one that returns to normal more quickly after exercise or exertion.

In practice, aerobic exercise means any exercise that makes you feel hot and sweaty and slightly breathless. This includes activities like walking, running, cycling, dancing, tennis, swimming or using any of the cardiovascular machines you may find in a gym, such as the stairwalker, treadmill, sky walker, rowing machine or stationary cycle.

The benefits of aerobic exercise are that it not only improves the strength of your heart, enabling it to do more for less effort, but also helps to burn off fat, which is vital if you are trying to control your weight. At the same time, it increases your body's demands for energy, enabling you to eat more food without getting fat. And, finally, it helps with appetite control, making it easier for you to control your food intake.

Strength

The second type of exercise you need for overall fitness is strengthening exercise. This is exercise that helps to make your muscles stronger, and this in turn helps to strengthen your bones and protects your joints from the risk of injury (because muscles protect the joints). This type of exercise is known as anaerobic exercise because it does not involve the muscles using oxygen as aerobic exercise does. It may involve the use of free weights and machines or any kind of exercise in which you use your own body weight to load the muscles – for example, press-ups, lunges and squats or some of the exercises involved in Pilates and yoga (see pages 34 and 58).

This type of exercise does not build up the fitness of your heart as aerobic exercise does. However, muscle is more active metabolically (that is, it burns more calories) than fat, so that, even at rest, the more muscle you have in relation to fat the more calories you will burn. This type of exercise is therefore excellent as an adjunct to aerobic exercise if you want to control your weight.

However, because it can cause a dramatic (although temporary) rise in blood pressure, anaerobic exercise is not recommended for people with uncontrolled high blood pressure or heart disease. If this applies to you, it is vital to check with your doctor before embarking on any kind of weight lifting or other anaerobic exercise programme.

exercising safely

If you have not exercised for some time, it is important to start gradually and build up slowly. If you have been sedentary, and especially if you are over 40 and/or have heart disease, heart-disease risk factors, a family history of heart disease or other chronic conditions such as arthritis, diabetes or a bad back, or are pregnant, check with your doctor before embarking on an exercise programme.

after a heart attack

If you are recovering from a heart attack or heart surgery, exercise can aid recovery and help you feel better quicker. It can also help to prevent further damage to your heart and blood vessels. Some hospitals, physiotherapists and/or doctors run rehabilitation programmes designed to improve your overall fitness, which may include advice on diet, exercise and stress management training. Such a programme can also help to restore damaged confidence, which is often a problem following a heart attack.

BELOW: Regular aerobic exercise, such as swimming and cycling, help strengthen the heart and lungs and keep you fit and healthy.

helping yourself

Suppleness

Suppleness exercises include any kind of exercise which involves stretching your muscles. It includes practices such as yoga or Pilates, a system of exercise that involves strengthening your body's central core, the abdomen and the back, together with other exercises to increase suppleness. There are a number of other simple stretching techniques which any fitness instructor or book on fitness will be able to teach you. Stretching helps to relax and lengthen muscles, which is especially important if you do any sort of strength work or weight training. In so doing, it encourages improved blood flow to the muscles, which in turn aids muscle healing. Yoga and Pilates are gentle forms of exercise which can be especially beneficial to people with heart problems as they help to calm the mind and body and reduce stress. However, there may still be some exercises or postures that are not recommended if you have heart disease, so be sure to check with your doctor before embarking on them and tell your instructor if you have high blood pressure or heart disease.

sample exercise programme

Here is a sample programme for someone who has built up to a reasonable level of fitness. It includes all the components of fitness – stamina, strength and suppleness. If you have heart disease or any other medical condition, check with your doctor before embarking on such a programme.

Mon	Gym – 1 hour (to include 30 min aerobic machines, 20 min weights and 10 min stretching)
Tues	Aerobics class or dance class
Wed	As Monday
Thurs	Pilates or yoga class
Fri	As Monday
Sat	Walk in the country/in-line skating/game of tennis, football or other sport
Sun	As Thursday

HOW MUCH EXERCISE SHOULD YOU DO?

Experts now recommend that you should aim to do some kind of moderate aerobic exercise, such as walking, swimming or cycling for 30 minutes, most days of the week. If you find it hard to do this amount of exercise in one session, you can split it up into shorter periods – for example, 15 minutes walking to the bus stop, 10 minutes walking in your lunch hour and 5 minutes climbing the stairs.

If you have previously been inactive, you may need to work up even to this level of activity. Let us take walking as an example, and show how you can build up over a period of two months. During weeks one and two, take a 10 minute walk (5 minutes each way), gradually increasing the speed at which you walk so that by the end of the second week you are walking further than you did at the beginning. In weeks three and four, increase your walk to 20 minutes (10 minutes each way) and proceed as before. During weeks five and six, increase your walk to 25 minutes (12½ minutes each way), proceeding as before. During weeks seven and eight, increase your walk to 30 minutes (15 minutes each way), proceeding as before.

You can apply the same principle to all sorts of aerobic activities, including cycling, swimming, skating, rowing and the various cardiovascular machines in the gym.

HOW INTENSELY SHOULD YOU EXERCISE?

For aerobic fitness, you need to work at between 60 and 75 per cent of your heart's maximum capacity. There are mathematical ways of working this out, which involve taking away your age from 220 to achieve your maximum heart rate and then calculating 60 to 75 per cent of that. There are also watches and other devices that can be attached to cardiovascular machines, which you can programme to monitor the rate at which you are working. Some have an alarm which bleeps if you exceed your maximum rate.

However, by and large, you should aim to be slightly out of breath, but not so breathless that you are unable to carry on a conversation, and feel hot and slightly sweaty, but not so exhausted that you feel you cannot go on. As a rule of thumb, you should feel that the effort you are applying is moderately hard.

MOVING ON

As you get fitter, you may get bored or find that your exercise becomes easy. You can then increase the complexity of what you do – for example, by including some hills in your walk or programming in some hills on the treadmill at the gym. You may also want start to include more complex activities such as dance, tennis or windsurfing, which involve working at a different pace for varying lengths of time. You will probably find that, once you get the exercise bug, you want to do more and more and may want to investigate more unusual types of exercise such as in-line skating or one of the many dance classes on offer these days.

do not exercise if:

- → **you experience chest pain –** **consult a doctor straight away.**
- → **you have uncontrolled high blood** **pressure.**
- → **your bones or joints are injured.**
- → **you have severe sunburn.**
- → **you have a severe hangover.**
- → **you feel sick or dizzy.**
- → **you experience swelling or sudden** **weight gain.**
- → **you are dehydrated.**
- → **it is excessively hot, humid or** **cold, or when air pollution levels** **are high if you have asthma or** **other lung problems.**
- → **you are being treated for a chronic** **medical condition without con-** **sulting your doctor.**

KEEPING AT IT

- → **Take it slowly** Too much too soon and you risk developing injuries or giving up because of pain or exhaustion. Always warm up for a few minutes before you start to exercise to warm the muscles.
- → **Pick an activity you enjoy** If you join a gym when you hate gyms, you are unlikely to keep up your exercise programme no matter how luxurious or well equipped the gym you join. The secret is to choose something else, perhaps a sport you always enjoyed at school, or try something unusual that you might never have thought of, like a flamenco class.
- → **Plan for setbacks** It can be difficult to plan in exercise, especially if you have a busy job or young family. Have a look at your daily timetable and find ways in which you might be able to fit in exercise. For example, get up an hour earlier, have a walk in the lunch hour or after work instead of going to the pub or get a friend to babysit while you go to the gym.
- → **Staying motivated** One of the best ways to keep up your enthusiasm is to join a class or to exercise with a friend. You are more likely to stick to your exercise

plan if you enlist the support of your friends and family, perhaps by organizing a family walk at the weekend.

- → **Pay attention to comfort** Wear loose, comfortable clothing that allows you to move easily and that absorbs sweat. There are many special fabrics that have been developed to wick sweat away from the body. However, until you develop the exercise habit it is just as easy to wear a loose T-shirt and a pair of loose cotton trousers. You should choose a good pair of 'cross training' shoes that support your heels and arches.
- → **Drink water** It is important to stay hydrated when you exercise in order to replace fluids lost in sweating. Take a bottle of water with you and take regular gulps, topping up as necessary.
- → **Listen to your body** Exercise can be a little uncomfortable, especially if you are not used to it, when you first start. But it should not be painful or totally exhausting. Your body is the best judge of how much you are capable of doing. Learn to listen to it and heed any warning signs (see box on page 32).

helping yourself

keeping a balance

Important as exercise and activity are, rest and relaxation are equally important components of a healthy lifestyle. Although many experts believe that stress is over-rated as a cause of heart disease, it can certainly do no harm to learn to relax and manage stress more effectively, especially because anxiety and other reactions to stress can affect the blood vessels and the heart.

THE 'FIGHT OR FLIGHT' REACTION

Whenever we face any sort of stress or threat, our bodies prepare themselves to face the threat by action – either by standing our ground and fighting the source of the threat or by running away from it. In these circumstances, the adrenal glands release stress hormones such as adrenaline (epinephrine), which among other things speed up the heart rate, release fats into the bloodstream to use as fuel, divert blood to the muscles and raise the blood pressure. This 'fight or flight' reaction as it is known served our cavemen ancestors well when they were facing a mammoth and had to kill it or run away. It is also perfectly functional in modern-day situations such as a marathon, a competitive tennis match or a situation of danger in which we literally have to run away.

However, in situations of mental stress, the chemicals released as a result of the fight or flight reaction are not discharged by physical activity. The heart pounds and the blood pressure remains persistently high, and the hormones and fats remain in the bloodstream where they may damage the lining of the arteries. Some doctors and scientists believe that this may accelerate the complex process described in Chapter 2, whereby atherosclerotic plaques are formed.

This may be especially damaging if you have other risk factors for heart disease, such as high blood pressure, or the sort of personality that reacts swiftly to stressful situations by becoming angry or hostile. Learning to control your physical reactions by learning physical relaxation methods, positive thinking and stress management techniques can be extremely worthwhile.

LISTENING TO YOUR BODY

The first step in learning to relax is to recognize when you are under stress. Although all of us react differently, there are some common signs and symptoms. These are listed in the column on the left.

Once you have identified the signs that you are under stress, you need to work out what is causing them. Different people have different triggers, and while major life events that you may not be able to do much about, such as a divorce, bereavement, job loss or financial problems, are

signs of stress:

→ aggravation of symptoms of heart disease or other chronic conditions you may suffer from, such as asthma or skin complaints like eczema.

→ anxiety.

→ appetite changes – comfort eating or being unable to eat.

→ cold, sweaty palms.

→ dry mouth or throat.

→ headaches and migraines.

→ insomnia – either being unable to drop off to sleep or waking up half-way through the night and being unable to fall asleep again.

→ irritability.

→ muscle tension.

→ outbursts of temper.

→ stomach upsets – nausea and vomiting or diarrhoea.

→ time pressure.

→ tiredness.

obviously stressful for everyone, there is also a wide range of more everyday events, such as being stuck in traffic, a row with your partner or having to meet a tight deadline at work, that can be equally stressful. Such day-to-day factors may ultimately even be more harmful because they are not one-off occurrences as major life events are.

Keeping a stress diary in which you note down stressful situations and your reaction to them can help you to identify the ones that are most stressful to you, so that you can begin to change your reaction to them.

LEARNING TO THINK POSITIVELY

Whenever you encounter any situation, a series of thoughts flashes across your mind, often without you being aware of them. If you do stop to listen to your thoughts for a moment or two, you might be surprised at how negative they are. For example, you join the gym and instead of focusing on how well you have done to take this positive step towards better health you criticize yourself for being fat and unfit and tell yourself you will never achieve anything. Such thoughts in themselves can be a source of stress.

Learning to replace the negative messages with more positive ones can do a great deal to alleviate stress. One way of doing this is to capture your thoughts by writing them down and then changing them to more positive ones. For instance, in the example above of joining a gym, you might write down things like 'I am a fat, lazy slob', 'I'll never succeed', 'I've never managed to stick to an exercise programme before, there's no reason why I should now'. The next step is to replace these thoughts with more reasonable, positive ones, such as 'This is the first step towards a new, healthier me', 'If I take it step by step and set myself goals I will succeed', 'If at first I don't succeed I'll try again'. Learn to regard set-backs and obstacles as opportunities to learn and see the good in situations rather than always looking for the bad.

This way of thinking may seem artificial at first, but once you get into the habit of thinking more positively and experience the benefits of not being so hard on yourself you will find that it begins to come naturally. After all, you would never castigate a friend in the way you do yourself. Now is the time to become your own best friend.

LEARNING TO RELAX

As well as positive thinking, there are several other ways in which you can reduce stress. One of the most useful is paying attention to the way you hold yourself and learning to consciously relax physically. Mental stress is often manifested in a taut, uncomfortable posture, tight muscles and shallow breathing. By consciously working on calming these physical signs, your body acts on your mind and helps to release stress. Indeed,

ABOVE: Keeping stress levels low can help the health of your heart. Laughter can be one of the best medicines.

BELOW: Yoga helps keep you supple, slows the heart rate and moderates breathing.

one of the benefits of regular exercise is that it helps to disperse stress hormones and helps your body to relax physically. There are also some more direct techniques you can use. Some of these, such as massage, yoga and meditation, are covered in Chapter 5, which deals with complementary therapies. Here we will look at a couple of simple relaxation techniques you can use at home or at work.

progressive relaxation

The idea behind this technique is that in order to relax your muscles you need to recognize how they feel when they are tense. It involves progressively tensing and then relaxing each major muscle group in turn, focusing on how the muscles feel when they are relaxed.

1	Breathe in and tighten your feet, calves and thighs. Really pull them as tight as you can and then breathe out and let them go.
2	Next tighten your abdomen, your buttocks and the muscles of your lower back, pulling them in as hard as you can. Then release and let them go.
3	Tighten your upper chest, shoulders, arms and hands. Clench them as hard as you can. Then, on an out-breath, let them go.
4	Finally, on an in-breath, tighten your neck and head, scrunch up your eyes and lips and feel your face go taut. Then breath out and let go, let your eyelids close gently, open your mouth and let your lips be slack, relax your jaw, feel the muscles in your scalp release.
5	Now you should be fully relaxed. Scan your body for any signs of tension and consciously relax. Stay sitting or lying fully relaxed for a few minutes. If any distracting thoughts enter your mind, do not dwell on them, simply let them go. When you are ready, wiggle your fingers and toes, open your eyes and bring yourself back to the present.

The following technique is useful at the end of your working day to help you wind down before you hit the road or rail, or to relax you when you get home, or indeed at any time you feel the need to relax and become calm.

Sit or lie quietly in a warm, quiet place and gently close your eyes or focus on a spot on the floor a few feet in front of you. If you are at home, you may want to take the phone off the hook or draw the blinds.	**1**
Gently relax each group of muscles, starting at your feet and working up through each major muscle group. You do not need to clench them as in the previous exercise.	**2**
Now focus on the flow of your breath in and out of your lungs. Feel the air expand your lungs as you breathe in, and notice how your lungs move down and your abdomen flattens as the air flows out. Do not force your breath, simply observe it.	**3**
Continue sitting in this way for ten minutes (or more if you have the time), staying relaxed and being aware of your breathing. If any noises or thoughts intrude, simply bring your attention back to your breathing. Some people find this easier if they mentally repeat a word or phrase such as 'peace', 'calm' or 'one', or the Indian mantra, 'om'.	**4**
After ten minutes or so, bring your attention back to the room you are in, notice external noises, the breeze from an open window, wiggle your fingers and toes, give yourself a stretch and slowly get up.	**5**

SLEEP

Insomnia, and the ensuing fatigue, is a common sign of stress. Getting a good night's sleep can help you to relax, both mentally and physically. Sleep forces your body to relax physically, and mentally it helps to recharge you so that you feel more positive and in control. Sleep may also play a more direct role in heart disease. Some research done in Mediterranean countries has shown that men who do not take a siesta are more prone to heart attack. The lesson is clear, you cannot beat a nap.

Different people need different amounts of sleep, and you will know how many hours you need to feel refreshed. If you suffer from insomnia or have trouble dropping off, try some of the following.

→ Establish a regular routine. No matter what time you go to bed, aim to get up at the same time.
→ Exercise, but not immediately before bedtime. Your half hour of moderate exercise will help to relax you physically.
→ Do not worry if you do not always get a full night's sleep. It is not the end of the world. The worst that is going to happen is that you will feel tired.
→ Do not go to bed hungry, but do not sleep on a heavy meal either. Have a light, easily digested meal early in the evening.

BELOW: **It's best to keep drinks that contain caffeine to the early part of the day if you want a good night's sleep.**

helping yourself

→ Cut down your intake of caffeine in tea, coffee and cola-type drinks, perhaps aiming to drink caffeine-containing drinks only early in the day. Substitute a calming herbal tea such as chamomile in the evening.

→ Watch the temperature of your bedroom and make sure it is neither too hot nor too cold. Most people prefer a temperature of 15–21°C (60–70°F).

→ Make sure your bedroom and bed are comfortable: banish the television, video and exciting books or music, look at your mattress and check it is not too hard or too soft , that your duvet is warm but not suffocating.

→ Do not drink alcohol before bedtime. Although it can make you feel sleepy initially, because it stimulates your nervous system you are likely to wake up later.

→ If you smoke – which you shouldn't if you are serious about protecting yourself against heart disease – do not have a cigarette before bedtime as it is a stimulant.

→ Establish a wind-down routine to help prime you for sleep. For example, a warm, calming bath, followed by a cup of chamomile tea or a warm drink.

developing healthier habits

As we have already seen, everyday habits like smoking, excessive alcohol intake and eating an unhealthy diet are inextricably linked to development of heart disease. The good news is that if you alter your habits you can lower or even rid yourself of your increased risk. No one is pretending that it is easy to kick the habits of a lifetime. However, the rewards you will gain in terms of improved overall health and a lower risk of heart disease are more than worth it. If at first you don't succeed, try again.

QUITTING SMOKING

The benefits of stopping smoking are tremendous. As well as reducing your risk of heart disease from the day you quit, you also help to reduce your risk of lung diseases such as cancer, emphysema and bronchitis. There are many other advantages too: you will have more money to spend on other things; your house, your breath, your clothes and your hair will no longer smell of smoke and you will save money on washing powders and dry cleaning bills; you will feel more energetic and have more stamina for exercise or other activities; and you will be helping to protect your friends and family from ill-health related to passive smoking.

There are many different ways to stop smoking. The key to success is to pick a method that is right for you. For example, if you are motivated by other people, enjoy company and like to please others, you may find

do you drink too much?

→ **Has your drinking ever caused you to be late for work or miss work?**

→ **Has your drinking ever caused you to neglect your family, friends or work commitments?**

→ **Has your drinking ever caused you to act in a way in which you would not normally behave – for example, more aggressively or sexually irresponsibly?**

→ **Has your drinking ever caused you to black out, or have you ever forgotten what happened during a night's drinking?**

→ **If you answered yes to any or all of these questions, it is time to pay attention to your drinking.**

encouragement and support by joining a stopping-smoking group. If you prefer to go it alone, you may find it helpful to buy a book or tape. Some people find it helpful to use a complementary therapy such as hypnosis, acupuncture or homeopathy (see Chapter 5), although you should bear in mind that these alone cannot quit for you but they can strengthen your resolve. In addition, there are now many aids your doctor can prescribe, such as nicotine patches that can help you quit more easily.

ALCOHOL

First the good news: experts agree that a moderate amount of alcohol can help to protect against heart disease by raising levels of protective HDL cholesterol and lowering the risk of blood clotting (see Chapter 6). However, regular heavy drinking (more than the number of recommended units, see panel right) or binge drinking can increase your risk. Heavy or binge drinking raises blood pressure, can trigger abnormal heart rhythms and causes weight gain, because alcoholic drinks are high in 'empty calories' – that is, calories that supply excess energy which is stored as fat, but do not provide nutrition – and may lead to diabetes. It can also lead to a condition known as cardiomyopathy, in which the heart muscles become large and flabby resulting eventually in heart failure.

Many people do not consider themselves to be heavy drinkers. Most of the time they may drink moderately or not at all. However, on a Friday night, on holiday or at a party or meal with friends they may easily get through a bottle or so of wine or a few measures of spirits. This can raise the blood pressure and, especially if you have atherosclerosis, can put you at risk of stroke and of atrial fibrillation, a rapid form of heart beat, which can increase the risk of both stroke and heart disease.

EATING A HEALTHIER DIET

Watching what you eat and changing from a high-fat diet to a low-fat one that contains plenty of fresh fruit and vegetables which actively help to protect you against heart disease is one of the most enjoyable steps you can take to reduce your risk and protect your heart and blood vessels. You will find full details of what foods to eat and what to avoid in Chapter 6, as well as a host of tempting recipes to help you on your way in Chapter 7.

illegal drugs

Illicit drugs, such as cocaine and amphetamines (speed), are becoming more commonly used. Both are stimulants that can speed up the heart rate, raise blood pressure and damage the heart. Although unusual, even a one-off use of such drugs can cause a heart attack and/or sudden death.

ABOVE: Regular heavy drinking can increase the risk of heart disease.

ways to moderate your drinking

→ **Never drink on an empty stomach. Always accompany an alcoholic drink with a light meal or snack.**

→ **Stick to your limits. Health professionals recommend that women should drink no more than three units of alcohol a day and men no more than four to reduce the risk of heart disease. A unit is equal to half a pint of regular strength beer or lager, one small glass of wine or a small (pub) measure of spirits.**

→ **Intersperse your drinks. When drinking socially, have a soft drink for every alcoholic drink you consume. Once you have had your daily quota of units, turn to soft or non-alcoholic drinks.**

This chapter covers all the various things you need to know about the orthodox medical approach to heart disease. It covers the **symptoms of heart disease**, how to get **a diagnosis**, the kinds of **tests that may be done** and the various types of **drugs and surgery** that may be used to treat heart disease.

When you are diagnosed with heart disease, **the approach your doctor takes** will depend on all sorts of factors, including your age, the state of your arteries, the severity of your symptoms and so on.

Many people can be treated, at least at first, by drug treatment. However, some people may eventually need to have surgery in the form of a **heart bypass operation or another procedure**. All these methods of treatment have a place in the management of heart disease, and your medical practitioner will try to devise the most appropriate regimen for you.

when to consult the doctor

Unfortunately, for many people the first intimation that they have developed heart disease is when they are rushed into hospital with a heart attack. In retrospect, many people who have a heart attack can recall experiencing symptoms which they either ignored or attributed to something else. For example, the pain of angina may sometimes be confused with indigestion.

Another reason why it can sometimes be difficult to diagnose heart disease is because symptoms are sometimes absent or vague. And just to complicate matters still further, some symptoms, such as breathlessness, can in certain circumstances be perfectly normal and not due to heart disease at all. For example, unless you are superfit it is perfectly normal to feel breathless when you climb a steep hill. What is not normal is to feel breathless when walking on the flat or when you are sitting. Women especially do not always experience classic symptoms of heart disease such as angina.

getting a diagnosis

The consultation with your doctor will have three distinct elements designed to help him or her to reach a diagnosis: your medical history, a physical examination and tests. The doctor will often be able to diagnose you from taking your medical history and doing a physical examination. However, in some cases the doctor may refer you to a consultant cardiologist (a specialist in heart disease) or a cardiac surgeon, who will have detailed knowledge and experience of treating heart disease.

YOUR MEDICAL HISTORY

The first part of your visit to the doctor will usually consist of your doctor asking you questions about your symptoms, when they occur and if there are any circumstances in which they are made worse or improve. The doctor will also want to know about your job, lifestyle, activity levels and diet, and will almost certainly also ask about your family medical history and whether there is a family history of heart disease. All these will enable him or her to decide which, if any, risk factors apply in your case.

THE PHYSICAL EXAMINATION

The doctor will take your pulse, measure your blood pressure, listen to your heart and lungs through a stethoscope and examine you for any

BELOW: Coronary angiography, in which an X-ray is used to view the coronary arteries, is one of the main diagnostic tests used to detect atherosclerosis.

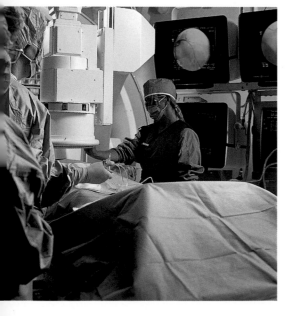

symptoms of heart disease

Although the following symptoms are by no means always due to heart disease and could be harmless or due to other medical conditions, if you experience any or all of them it would be a good idea to make an appointment to see your doctor.

→ **Unusual breathlessness** when doing light activity or at rest, or breathlessness that comes on suddenly.

→ **Angina** – chest pain, heaviness or tightness in the chest that comes on during activity or emotional stress and may spread to the arms, neck, jaw, face, back or stomach.

→ **Palpitations** – awareness of your heart beat or a feeling of having a rapid and unusually forceful heart beat, especially if it lasts for several hours or recurs over several days and/or causes chest pain, breathlessness or dizziness.

→ **Fainting** – although not always a serious symptom, fainting (or syncope to use the medical term) is due to insufficient oxygen reaching the brain, which may be because of atherosclerosis so you should report it to your doctor.

→ **A bluish tinge to the fingernails or around the lips** (known medically as cyanosis) can be a result of too little oxygen in the blood.

→ **Fluid retention or puffiness** (oedema to use the correct medical term) is abnormal accumulation of fluid in tissues such as ankles, legs, chest or abdomen. Although usually perfectly normal, for example on a hot day, it can be a sign of heart failure.

→ **Fatigue** can have numerous other causes, including depression. However, especially if combined with other suspicious symptoms, it is grounds for seeing the doctor.

Important note:
Severe crushing chest pain that may come on at rest and is accompanied by sweating, light-headedness, nausea or shortness of breath and lasts more than 15 minutes is probably a heart attack. Seek medical help immediately.

potential signs of heart disease, such as a bluish tinge to your fingernails or oedema. These simple tests can be carried out in the doctor's surgery. He or she may then refer you for more specialized tests or cardiac investigations.

TESTS FOR HEART DISEASE

Cardiac tests are designed to determine whether you have heart disease and to rule out other possible causes for your symptoms. They may also be used to monitor your condition if you have already been diagnosed with heart disease, to enable the doctor to forecast how your condition may progress and to decide the most appropriate treatment. The tests shown in the panel on page 46 are those most likely to be used. Although there are a lot of them, bear in mind that you may only need one or two. Some of the tests may be combined to provide a fuller picture of your condition.

TEST	WHAT IT IS	WHY IT IS DONE
Electrocardiogram (ECG)	**Small metal electrodes taped to your arms, legs and chest are connected by wires to a recording machine (electrocardiograph) which detects and amplifies electrical signals from your heart.**	**To check the rhythm and electrical activity of your heart.** Variation: exercise ECG or exercise stress test, which is performed while you are walking on a treadmill or cycling on a stationary bicycle. It is used to check whether chest pain or discomfort on exertion is a result of heart disease.
Holter monitoring	**A special type of ECG in which your heart is monitored continuously over 24 hours using a portable recording device. You are asked to record activities and symptoms in a diary so that any episodes can be checked against the activity of your heart at those times.**	**To help diagnose symptoms such as palpitations and silent ischaemia.**
Echocardiogram	**A type of ultrasound scan in which a transducer is placed on your chest wall. This picks up echoes from your heart, which are displayed on a monitor to build up a picture of different parts of your heart in motion.**	**To check the size, function and thickness of your heart muscle and the function of the heart valves.** Variations: Doppler echocardiography, which measures the speed of blood flow through your heart chambers, and trans-oesophageal echocardiography, in which you swallow a small probe which takes 'pictures' of your heart.
Radionuclide tests	**A small, harmless amount of a radioactive marker or isotope is injected, often while you are exercising on a stationary bicycle or treadmill. The isotope emits gamma rays, which can be picked up by a special camera, and the images are analyzed by computer. There are two main types: technetium and thallium scans.**	**To examine the inside of the heart as it empties and fills and/or to examine blood flow to the heart.**
Magnetic resonance imaging (MRI)	**A type of scan in which you lie in a 'drum' which contains a magnet. Magnetic fields and radio waves create an image of soft tissues such as the heart and arteries.**	**To measure blood flow through major arteries and detect abnormal heart function.**
Cardiac enzyme tests	**A blood test that measures enzymes released by the heart muscles when it is damaged in a heart attack.**	**To detect the amount of damage the heart has sustained in a heart attack. Samples are taken over a few days.**
Cardiac catheterization (catheter investigation or catheter test) and coronary angiography	**A small tube (catheter) is inserted into a vein or artery in the groin or arm under local anaesthetic and used to produce an angiogram (a moving X-ray) of the coronary arteries and other parts of the heart.**	**To check where arteries have narrowed and how narrow they have become, and to check blood pressure within the heart and the functioning of parts of the heart.**
Electrophysiological tests	**Fine tubes called electrode catheters inserted through a vein, usually in the groin, are moved to the heart where they stimulate it and record the electrical impulses.**	**To diagnose abnormal heart rhythms, pinpoint which area is affected and establish whether medication is effective.**

drug treatment for heart disease

A tremendous number of different drugs are used to treat or prevent heart disease and to control the associated symptoms or risk factors such as angina or high blood pressure. They are designed to correct the faulty function of the heart or circulation, and some may benefit you in several different ways. However, by and large, they fall into a handful of main types which act in similar ways (see table). This means that, if a particular drug does not suit you, the doctor will usually be able to prescribe a different drug within the same category that may suit you better. It is worth bearing in mind that there may be a period of trial and error before the right drug for you is found. Be patient and report any side-effects to your doctor.

Most of the drugs you are likely to be prescribed for heart disease are tablets or capsules that are taken by mouth. However, there are a few

drugs you may be prescribed

In the panel below is a run-down of the main groups of drugs that may be used to treat heart disease and associated conditions, in alphabetical order, outlining how they work and some of their common side-effects. It is intended purely as a general guide. For further specific information on any drugs that have been prescribed for you, contact your doctor or pharmacist.

ACE INHIBITORS

Examples: captopril, enalapril, lisinopril

ACE (short for angiotensin-converting enzyme) inhibitors are used to treat and prevent heart failure and to lower high blood pressure. They work by blocking the activity of a hormone called angiotensin-II, which narrows the blood vessels, so opening up the blood vessels, improving blood flow and decreasing the amount of work the heart has to do. They are especially useful to treat blood pressure in people with diabetes, but they are less effective for people of African-Caribbean origin.

SIDE-EFFECTS

Although generally well tolerated, they can cause a dramatic drop in blood pressure, especially when first used by people who are taking diuretics. They can also impair kidney function in people with kidney disease, and for this reason the doctor should start you on a low dose and check your blood pressure and kidney function when first prescribing them. Some ACE inhibitors cause changes in taste, skin rashes, a dry irritating cough and very occasionally a severe allergic reaction. If this happens, contact the doctor immediately.

ANGIOTENSIN-II RECEPTOR ANTAGONISTS

Example: losartan

A fairly new type of drug used to lower blood pressure by limiting angiotensin, a hormone produced by the body which regulates blood pressure. They work on the kidneys, adrenal glands, heart, brain and sympathetic nervous system.

SIDE-EFFECTS

Because they are new, not so much is known about angiotensin-II receptor antagonists, but they seem to avoid many of the side-effects associated with other classes of blood-pressure-lowering drugs, except for dizziness.

questions to ask the doctor (if you are prescribed blood-pressure-lowering drugs)

→ What is my blood pressure now?
→ What should the appropriate blood pressure for my age be?
→ How often should I have my blood pressure measured?
→ What type of medication has been prescribed?
→ What side-effects might I experience?
→ What else can I do to help lower my blood pressure?

other ways of taking or being given drugs, including under the tongue (sublingually), in spray form, as patches or as an injection into a muscle, into a vein or under the skin.

How well a particular drug works and the way it affects you depends on several factors, such as your age, your sex, your weight, your genetic make-up and any other health problems you may also have. Your doctor will take all these factors into account when devising a medication regimen.

the orthodox approach

SIDE-EFFECTS AND LIMITATIONS

A drug is any substance that changes your body's chemistry and how it works. For this reason all drugs, including ones you buy over-the-counter and 'natural' herbal remedies, will have potential risks as well as benefits. In prescribing any drug, the doctor has to weigh up potential risks against the benefits and to prescribe the drugs that are likely to be most effective and safe for you.

ANTI-ARRHYTHMIC DRUGS

Examples: amiodarone, digoxin, flecainide, propafenone

As the name suggests, these are drugs that control the rhythm of your heart. It is particularly important to follow the instructions for taking any anti-arrhythmic drug you may be prescribed to the letter, as the effectiveness of these drugs depends on keeping exactly the right amount in your bloodstream.

SIDE-EFFECTS

Anti-arrhythmic drugs are usually well tolerated. However, all of those prescribed may cause side-effects and in some cases may even worsen heart rhythm abnormalities. For this reason, in some circumstances the doctor may first give the drugs in hospital so that any untoward effects can be monitored. You should always report any side-effects to the doctor and make sure that he or she knows about any other drugs you have been prescribed.

ANTICOAGULANTS

Examples: heparin, warfarin

These are used to inhibit blood clotting by preventing fibrin (a protein involved in clotting) from forming. They are also used to treat deep vein thromboses (clots in the legs) and to prevent these from travelling to the lungs where they may cause a pulmonary embolism (blood clot on the lungs). Anticoagulants may be administered in different ways. Warfarin, for example, is taken orally for long-term prevention of

clotting. It is most often used for people with valvular heart disease or with heart rhythm abnormalities. Heparin is usually given by injection into a vein when it necessary to prevent clotting immediately. A newer form of heparin can be given by injection under the skin (subcutaneously) for longer.

SIDE-EFFECTS

Everyone prescribed anticoagulants should be issued with an 'anticoagulant card' which contains details of the dose. Because anticoagulants prevent fibrin from forming they can also cause or aggravate bleeding, so you will need regular blood tests to make sure the blood's clotting activity is kept within safe limits. You should also make sure the doctor and/or pharmacist knows you are taking anticoagulants before taking other medications (either prescription drugs or over-the-counter remedies) because they can interact with a variety of these, including antibiotics and aspirin.

ANTICOAGULANT WATCH

Report any of the following to your doctor as they could be a sign that the dose of anticoagulants prescribed is too high:

→ **Prolonged bleeding from cuts, grazes and other minor injuries**
→ **Bleeding that does not stop by itself.**
→ **Bleeding from the gums.**
→ **Nose bleeds lasting more than a few minutes.**
→ **Red or dark brown urine or faeces.**
→ **Heavier than usual menstrual bleeding or other vaginal bleeding.**

designer drugs for heart disease

Our individual genetic make-up very largely determines how our bodies react to different drugs. With recent breakthroughs in genetic science, it is anticipated that within the next few years doctors will be able to prescribe drugs that are tailored to you individually and that therefore do not have side-effects. Thus it will be possible for doctors to prescribe the right drug, for the right person, first time.

LEFT: Your doctor will try to prescribe the right drugs for you with fewest side-effects.

ASPIRIN AND ANTIPLATELET DRUGS

Examples: aspirin, clopidogrel, ticlopidine

Aspirin and other antiplatelet drugs prevent blood clotting by reducing the stickiness of the blood cells called platelets which are involved in clotting. They are used to lower the risk of death after a heart attack or stroke, for people with angina and to prevent blood clotting following bypass surgery and other procedures.

SIDE-EFFECTS

Aspirin is one of the safest, most tried and tested drugs, and side-effects are few. They include indigestion, nausea, vomiting and constipation, although these can be minimized by using coated preparations that buffer the effects of the drug. They may also irritate the lining of the stomach, causing bleeding, and occasionally trigger an asthma attack.

BETA BLOCKERS

Examples: atenolol, oxprenolol, propranolol

These long-established drugs partially block the effects of the stress hormones adrenaline (epinephrine) and noradrenaline (norepinephrine), which make the heart beat faster and more forcefully. They are used to prevent angina attacks and to lower high blood pressure and reduce the risk of a subsequent heart attack in people who have already had one. Some beta blockers help to control abnormal heart rhythms.

SIDE-EFFECTS

There are a whole range of minor side-effects which vary from one type of beta blocker to another, but they are usually mild. They include light-headedness, pins and needles, cold fingers and toes, stomach upsets, depression, nightmares, wheezing, drowsiness, lethargy, weakness, fatigue and visual disturbances. In people with diabetes who are on medication, beta blockers can mask symptoms of low blood glucose (hypoglycaemia). They should also be used with caution in people with heart failure. You should never stop taking beta blockers suddenly, as this can worsen angina. Your doctor will advise you how to tail them off gradually if you need to stop taking them for any reason.

CALCIUM CHANNEL BLOCKERS, OR CALCIUM ANTAGONISTS

Examples: amlopidine, diltiazem, nifedipine, verapamil

Calcium is needed for the action of muscle cells in the heart. Calcium antagonists reduce the amount of calcium entering the muscle cells of the arteries and thus relax the muscles in the arteries causing them to dilate (widen). This in turn increases blood flow to the heart, reducing the workload of the heart and lowering blood pressure. They may be used to treat angina and/or to reduce high blood pressure. Different calcium antagonists work in slightly different ways. For example, some like nifedipine increase the heart rate at rest, while others like verapamil reduce the natural speeding up of the heart rate when you exercise.

the orthodox approach

Many of the drugs used to treat heart disease have minor side-effects – that is, other effects that arise from taking the drug in addition to its therapeutic action – although harmful side-effects are rare. The doctor and/or the pharmacist from whom you pick up your prescription should inform you about any side-effects that you may expect to experience. The drug information leaflet enclosed with your medication should also outline potential side-effects. Although it can be somewhat alarming to see all these written down, do remember that, firstly, you are unlikely to experience all the side-effects mentioned and may not experience any at all, and that, secondly, side-effects often subside once your body has adjusted to the drug. If you do develop side-effects – that is, any unusual symptoms or new problems – following the prescription of a new medication, tell your doctor. In any case, the doctor will usually want to monitor you carefully when you first start on a particular drug.

SIDE-EFFECTS

These include flushing, headache, ankle swelling, fatigue, nausea, dizziness, palpitations, drowsiness, insomnia, stomach upsets, rashes and tinnitus (ringing in the ears). Despite the length of the list, these are usually mild and serious side-effects are uncommon.

DIURETICS

Examples: bendrofluazide, chlorthalidone

There are many different diuretics, or 'water tablets', but they all work on the kidneys to increase excretion of water and salt in the urine. They are useful for treating heart failure, which causes an excess of water and salt in the body's tissues, and for reducing blood pressure. There are various types of diuretics, some of which can cause potassium to be lost from the bloodstream. The doctor will arrange a blood test a few weeks after prescribing these to check that your potassium levels have not dropped too low. If they have you will be prescribed potassium supplements or a potassium-sparing diuretic.

SIDE-EFFECTS

You may find you need to urinate more often, especially when diuretics are first prescribed. If this becomes troublesome you should report it to your doctor. Other side-effects may include loss of appetite, stomach upsets, dehydration, increased blood cholesterol, allergic reactions (in people with asthma), increased uric acid levels (with a consequent risk of gout) and a rise in blood glucose, which may be significant in people with diabetes. If you are on diuretics it is important not to limit your consumption of salty foods as this can counteract the diuretic effect.

LIPID-LOWERING DRUGS

Examples: fluvastatin, lovastatin, simvastatin

These drugs are designed to lower levels of blood fats or lipids. They may work by raising levels of good HDL cholesterol or lowering circulating amounts of bad LDL cholesterol. The main type are known as statins, cholesterol-lowering drugs that inhibit the action of an enzyme involved in cholesterol synthesis and can lower LDL cholesterol levels by a fifth or more. Where statins are not appropriate (do not use them if you have liver disease or are pregnant or breastfeeding), other drugs may be prescribed. Lipid-lowering drugs should be used in conjunction with lifestyle measures designed to lower cholesterol.

SIDE-EFFECTS

Statins are generally well tolerated, but they may cause stomach upsets, muscle pains and weakness. They can also interact with fibrates (another lipid-lowering drug) causing muscle pains. Some statins may cause liver problems or cataracts, so you may need liver function tests and regular eye examinations.

medication checklist

→ Check to make sure you understand why the doctor has prescribed any drug you are using and what its effects are likely to be.

→ Check on the dose of the drug, and when and how often you need to take it. Some drugs, for example some of those used for angina, are only taken when the symptom develops.

→ If you are taking several different types of tablets, it is possible to get special dispensers into which you put your daily drugs for morning and evening.

→ Check the instructions on how the drug should be taken. For example, whether it is to be taken with water, with food or between meals.

→ Check the pack for any special instructions, such as whether or not the drug may be taken with alcohol.

→ Check with your doctor of pharmacist if you are in doubt about any aspect of the medication you have been prescribed.

→ Never share any drug you have been prescribed with anyone else. Remember, it has been prescribed for you and your symptoms.

→ Keep all heart drugs in a safety medicine cabinet well out of reach of children.

→ Do not keep any medication beyond its use-by date.

NITRATES

Examples: glyceryl trinitrate, isosorbide dinitrate, isosorbide mononitrate

Nitrates relax the muscles in the walls of the blood vessels, so reducing the workload of the heart's left ventricle. They are used to alleviate anginal pain and to prevent 'stable' angina (see page 19), although they may become progressively less effective over time. They come in the form of sublingual tablets which you allow to dissolve under your tongue, as an aerosol spray which you spray under your tongue, in tablet form to be taken orally and as skin patches to prevent angina. Because the patches may become less effective if worn continuously, the doctor may advise leaving them off for several hours a day.

SIDE-EFFECTS

These include flushing, a throbbing headache, dizziness and faintness. These effects tend to be most troublesome with the tablet form of nitrate and to wane with continued use.

POTASSIUM CHANNEL ACTIVATORS

Example: nicorandil

These are another type of drug that, like nitrates, act to relax the walls of the coronary arteries and improve blood flow. They are used to alleviate angina. Unlike nitrates, they appear to be effective even with continued use.

SIDE-EFFECTS

These are similar to those for nitrates and include headache, flushing, indigestion and dizziness.

THROMBOLYTIC DRUGS, OR 'CLOT BUSTERS'

Examples: anistreplase, streptokinase

Administered after a heart attack, thrombolytic drugs can dramatically reduce the risk of death. They work by breaking up clots, restoring blood flow through the narrowed artery and reducing damage to the heart muscles. The most common clot buster, streptokinase, is given directly into a vein and can transform a potentially severe heart attack into a relatively mild one.

SIDE-EFFECTS

Because thrombolytic drugs, by their very nature, dissolve clots there can be a risk of serious bleeding. If you have recently had surgery or have a high risk of bleeding for any reason the doctor will not prescribe them. If you have been given thrombolytic drugs, you will be given a card to carry with you detailing the type of drug given and when. This is because, if the drug administered was streptokinase or anistreplase, it is important not to give it again for several years. If you have another heart attack a different thrombolytic will be given.

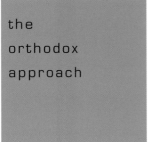

the

orthodox

approach

non-drug treatment for heart disease

Most people with heart disease can have their condition controlled effect-ively with drugs. However, in some instances – for example, if your blood vessels have become very narrowed or if drug treatment alone is not controlling your angina – the consultant may recommend a 'revascularization' procedure to open up narrowed blood vessels or replace blocked arteries by means of a 'heart bypass'. The surgeon will usually perform an angiogram (cardiac catheterization) to check on the state of your blood vessels before recommending this course of action.

REVASCULARIZATION PROCEDURES

CORONARY ANGIOPLASTY

This is a procedure in which the fatty build-up (atheroma) in the narrowed artery is compressed against the artery walls, opening them up so more blood can flow through. The operation, performed under local anaesthetic, involves passing a catheter with a deflated 'balloon' on the end into an artery in the groin or the arm and using X-ray guidance to steer it to the section of narrowed artery. The sausage-shaped balloon is then inflated, compressing the atheroma, and then deflated and removed. This is known as balloon angioplasty. Another form of angioplasty uses a stent, a short stainless steel mesh tube, which is then left in place to help hold the vessel open. There are also other newer methods of performing angioplasty involving lasers and ultrasound.

CORONARY BYPASS SURGERY

The narrowed sections of the coronary arteries are bypassed by grafting a blood vessel, either a vein from your leg or the internal mammary artery that runs down the inside of the chest wall, between the aorta – the main artery from the heart – and a point beyond the narrowed area. A bypass graft can be performed for each of the heart's four arteries. This is why you may hear it referred to as a single, double, triple or quadruple bypass operation.

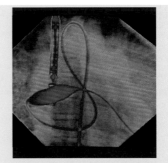

LEFT: Balloon angioplasty – shown here on an angiogram (X-ray of the arteries) – is used to restore blood flow in arteries blocked by atheroma.

KEYHOLE CORONARY SURGERY

Microsurgery, or 'keyhole' surgery to use its popular name, is sometimes used and may lead to fewer complications and a faster recovery. It may also make it possible for people to return to work and other activities faster than after conventional heart surgery. However, it is not appropriate for everyone who needs heart surgery.

TRANSMYOCARDIAL LASER REVASCULARIZATION

This is a fairly new procedure in which a small incision is made in the chest and a laser beam used to create up to 40 small channels through the heart wall, allowing the heart muscle (the myocardium) to fill with blood and oxygen from the ventricles. Unlike other types of heart surgery, which treat the coronary arteries, this technique treats the heart itself

recovering from heart surgery

→ Bear in mind that recovery can take varying lengths of time, depending on the severity of your condition, your age and your overall health.

→ Expect to feel emotionally fragile and easily fatigued for at least the first three to six months, and take life easy.

→ Pain in the chest, neck, back and arms is normal when you are recovering from heart surgery. However, if you are worried contact your doctor.

→ You should not drive your car for at least a month after bypass surgery. Special rules apply to heavy goods and other commercial licences. Contact the licensing authority for details.

→ Memory loss affects some people after heart surgery. Be patient, it usually passes about six months after the operation.

→ Check with your doctor when you can return to work. By and large, with an office job you may be able to return after two months, or if you have a physical job you will be advised to wait at least three months for healing to complete.

→ Ask your doctor when you can resume sex. Most advise waiting about a month.

→ Ask your doctor whether there is a cardiac rehabilitation and/or heart support programme in your area that you can enroll on.

HEART TRANSPLANTATION

This involves removing a person's heart and replacing it with a healthy heart from a donor. Sometimes a lung transplant is done at the same time – a heart-lung transplant. In the past, heart transplants sometimes failed because the person's immune system rejected the transplanted heart. However, with the use of drugs to prevent rejection, heart transplants are now extremely successful, although a shortage of donors means that a heart transplant is usually only recommended for someone with advanced heart disease.

RIGHT: Various kinds of open heart surgery may be performed to bypass arteries that have become blocked or narrowed, correct disorders of heart valves, and to transplant a new heart.

VALVULAR SURGERY

If you have valvular problems you may have mitral valvuloplasty (balloon treatment) to stretch a damaged mitral valve, valve surgery in the form of valve replacement or valve repair and microsurgery, which may produce fewer complications.

PACEMAKERS

If you have problems with the electrical impulses in your heart causing a 'heart block', you may have an artificial pacemaker implanted. This consists of a pulse generator programmed to deliver electrical impulses to your heart attached to two electrode leads. In transvenous implantation, a lead is inserted under local anaesthetic via a vein at the shoulder or the base of the neck and under X-ray guidance propelled into the correct chamber of the heart. The lead is attached to the pacemaker, which is fitted into a small pocket between the skin and the chest muscle. In epicardial implantation, the electrode lead is attached to the outer surface of the heart, or epicardium, and the pacemaker itself implanted under the skin of the abdomen.

A pacemaker may also be recommended if you have irregularities of heart rhythm to help maintain a steady beat.

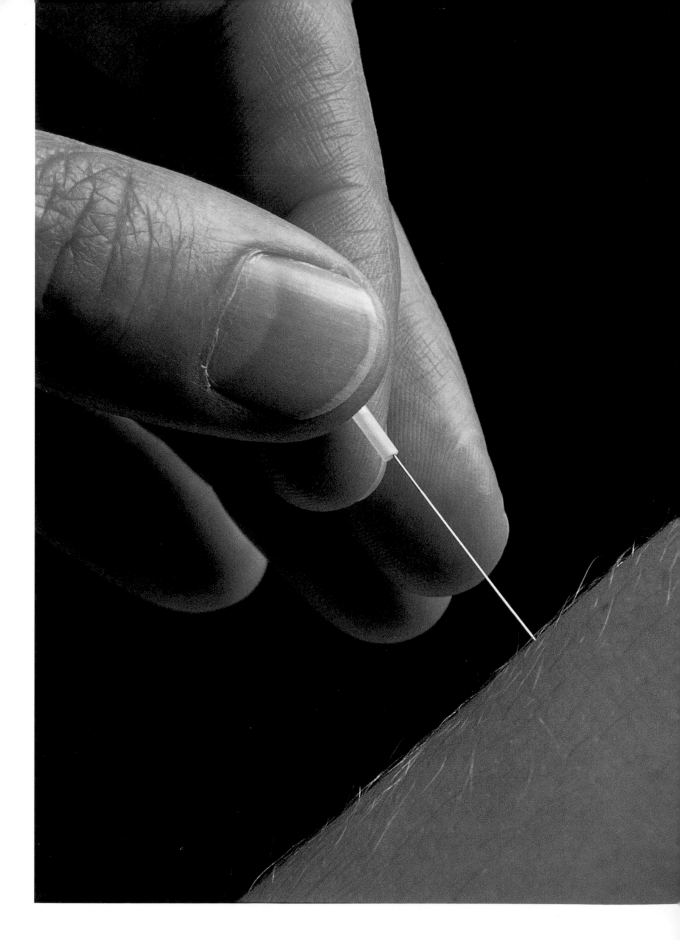

Complementary therapies have much to offer in the treatment and prevention of heart disease. If you have already been diagnosed with heart disease or have had a heart attack, it can help you to **think more positively about yourself and your illness**. It can also help you to relax and may ease some symptoms, such as angina.

If you want to avoid heart disease or prevent symptoms from progressing, complementary treatments can be valuable in helping you to **take a close look at your lifestyle and take positive steps to improve it**.

There is a tremendous range of complementary therapies to choose from. In fact, some complementary relaxation techniques such as yoga and meditation may even be included on rehabilitation programmes to help **relieve stress and lower blood pressure**.

Having said that, it is important to bear in mind that complementary treatments are designed to be **an adjunct to orthodox treatment** and not to replace it. You should always make sure that your orthodox doctor knows about any complementary treatments you plan to try, in case they may interact with an orthodox treatment you have been prescribed.

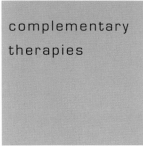

complementary
therapies

advantages of complementary therapy

When you have heart disease or any other condition that cannot be cured, you will have to follow the advice of your doctor and other health professionals for the rest of your life in order to stay healthy. This can understandably make you feel as if your life is not in your own hands.

One tremendous benefit of complementary medicine is that it allows you to be active in helping yourself, so helping you to feel more in control over your condition and its outcome.

Complementary therapists, whatever their speciality, tailor their treatments very much to you as an individual. This means that the precise nature of the treatment recommended will vary depending on your medical history, your symptoms and your lifestyle. Complementary treatments are holistic – that is, they look at you as a whole person and

HYPNOTHERAPY

Hypnotherapy is a kind of psychotherapy which acts on the subconscious mind to change thought and behaviour patterns. During hypnotherapy, the therapist induces a trance-like state of deep relaxation somewhere between waking and sleeping. During a hypnotic trance, breathing, heart rate and metabolism can be slowed.

There are a tremendous number of different methods the practitioner may use to induce a hypnotic trance. One of the most familiar is to ask you to concentrate on a real or imagined object while the practitioner suggests that with each out-breath you feel ever more relaxed. He or she may then ask you to imagine a beautiful scene to encourage your mind to release its conscious hold on the external environment. The therapist will usually encourage you to learn self-hypnosis which you can use at home.

Hypnotherapy can help people with heart disease in many ways. Because it is deeply relaxing, it can help to control conditions like high blood pressure. It can also be used to help you acquire healthier lifestyle habits.

Hypnohealing, a variety of hypnotherapy, is aimed at healing disease by encouraging you to visualize a symptom such as the pain of angina, for example, and to imagine it being banished from your body. The technique is used in pain clinics to help people reduce their dependence on drug treatments for chronic pain.

RELAXATION AND VISUALIZATION

Relaxation and visualization are two separate disciplines which are often combined. Many of us think of relaxation as a passive process, but true relaxation is not passive at all. It involves actively turning your attention to controlling and resolving the effects of stress. In fact, it can often take quite a lot of effort to learn to relax, especially if you are prone to anxiety or nervousness or always on the go.

Therapists may use a variety of techniques to help you to relax. One of the most common is visualization, a technique which has its roots in the Eastern practice of meditation. It often involves imagining a special place, such as a beautiful garden, a beach or a beautiful room, when you are relaxed in order to deepen your relaxation and allow your mind to let go. The therapist will encourage you to use all your senses to explore the place, feel the sun on your body, hear the wind rustling in the trees, see the blue of the sky and the yellow of the sand.

Relaxation and visualization work to rebalance the body's autonomic nervous system that controls our heartbeat, circulation and breathing and the adrenal glands that release stress hormones such as adrenaline (epinephrine) so helping to slow the heartbeat, relax the blood vessels, lower blood pressure and slow breathing.

Both techniques are particularly safe, which makes them useful for someone recovering from a heart attack.

not just a set of symptoms. Complementary practitioners will usually have more time to spend talking to you than the average orthodox doctor.

active approaches

Autogenic training, hypnotherapy, relaxation and visualization, tai chi and yoga are a group of therapies that all involve some sort of active participation on your part. In many of them, this involves controlling your breathing. Although they are all different, another thing they have in common is that they reflect the belief that the mind and the body work together as one unit. This belief, which underlies many Eastern therapies, has been given a new lease of life recently by the new scientific discipline of psychoneuroimmunology, which studies the chemical links between our feelings and bodily symptoms.

BELOW: A range of mind-body therapies can be used to help alleviate stress.

AUTOGENIC TRAINING

Autogenic training takes the principles of Eastern meditation and reinterprets them in a way that is easier for the Western mind to understand. The idea is that automatic functions like breathing, blood circulation and blood pressure can be regulated by the mind. It involves learning a series of simple mental exercises designed to switch off the 'fight or flight' response, which as we have seen constricts the blood vessels, speeds up the heart rate and raises blood pressure.

Autogenic training may be done on a one-to-one basis or in a group. The autogenic practitioner will teach you two sets of exercises designed to relax the mind and the body. The first uses key phrases or suggestions, such as 'My arms are warm and heavy', in order to concentrate the mind on the physiological changes that occur when the body relaxes. The second group of exercises, which are practised at home, concentrate on releasing emotional and physical stress directly, for example by shouting, crying or punching a pillow.

Autogenic training has been shown in several clinical trials to relieve many stress-linked conditions, including high blood pressure. One study, carried out in 1988, took 90 patients with high blood pressure and divided them into two groups, half of whom were given autogenic training and half of whom were not. The results found that those who had autogenic training experienced a fall in blood pressure comparable to that seen in patients given regular antihypertensive medication. Patients with mild hypertension seemed to respond best.

complementary therapies

TAI CHI

Tai chi (or tai chi chuan to give it its full name) is a non-combative martial art system that includes meditation and exercises designed to enhance health. It is part of a complete system of Oriental medicine that includes acupuncture, acupressure, herbal medicine and massage.

The basis of tai chi is practice of a set of slow-moving, graceful exercises performed in a set order, designed to encourage general relaxation and harmony between the mind, body and spirit known as 'the form'. According to Eastern thinking, this helps to rebalance and encourage the flow of *chi*, the body's invisible lifeforce.

The practice, which may be learnt one-to-one or more often in a class of 15 to 30 people, usually takes place indoors in the West. However, in China it is traditional to practise near trees so the person can absorb the energy given off by the trees.

Tai chi is a gentle art that is safe whatever your age or level of fitness. This makes it especially useful for stress-linked problems such as anxiety, tension, high blood pressure and circulatory problems. It can also assist in rehabilitation after a heart attack.

YOGA

Yoga – Sanskrit for 'union' – is a gentle system that aims to unite body, mind and spirit through a series of postures, or *asanas*, together with breathing techniques and meditation, all designed to relax the muscles, improve suppleness and enhance the physical functioning of the body.

There are many different forms of yoga, but most of those taught in the West are based on hatha yoga, a gentle system which concentrates on the *asanas*. These are performed in a particular sequence so as to exercise all your muscle groups, encourage healthy circulation and flush toxins from the body.

Yoga is usually taught in classes of around 15 to 20 people, which usually last for 1 or 2 hours. The teacher will usually ask if anyone has any health problems, but if he or she does not, you should draw any problems you have to his or her attention. Some practitioners will give one-to-one sessions to people with particular medical problems.

Yoga is helpful for any stress-related conditions such as anxiety, high blood pressure, and circulatory and heart problems. There are a vast number of classes on offer. When looking for a class, you should aim to find one that stresses the relaxing benefits of yoga. Although generally safe, some of the more dynamic forms of yoga, such as Iyengar and Astanga yoga, are unsuitable for people with heart and circulatory problems.

manipulative therapies

We all instinctively rub an injury to stop it hurting, and the use of the healing power of touch is one of the world's most ancient healing techniques. Manipulative therapies such as massage, osteopathy and reflexology involve the practitioner using the power of touch to work directly on your body to alleviate pain, improve circulation, relax you and restore health.

RIGHT: Massage is relaxing and soothing, and helps calm the heart.

MASSAGE

Massage involves manipulating the body's soft tissues to promote and restore mental and physical health. It forms the basis of other complementary therapies, such as aromatherapy and shiatsu, and plays a vital role in Chinese and Ayurvedic medicine.

There are many different types of massage. Some, like shiatsu and reflexology, work on pressure or reflex points – points on the body or feet, which are said to correspond to the various bodily organs – and rely on the principle of rebalancing the flow of *chi*, the body's vital force. Others are used to alleviate specific conditions. One thing they all have in common is that they are supremely relaxing, improve breathing patterns, lower the heart rate and blood pressure, and improve circulation. This makes them especially useful for stress and stress-linked conditions such as circulatory problems. Because it is both gentle and safe, massage is often used to help people recovering from heart attacks or heart surgery.

Many of the various types of massage involve a set of common techniques including stroking, kneading, pressure knuckling and pummelling. The therapist may use essential oils, which according to aromatherapists have healing qualities by acting on the limbic system – the part of the brain concerned with emotion.

OSTEOPATHY

Osteopathy, a system of healing dating back to the 19th century, is a complete system of diagnosis and treatment that involves the practitioner working on the body's structure – that is, the skeleton, muscles, ligaments and connective tissue. Although many of us think of osteopathy as primarily for back pain, it can also be tremendously useful for a wide range of other conditions, including high blood pressure.

There are many different techniques. They include soft tissue manipulation, which is very similar to massage, to encourage muscular relaxation and calm the mind, and indirect techniques used to relieve tension in stressed tissue by gentle palpation.

Practitioners of visceral osteopathy diagnose and treat heart and lung problems by gently palpating the abdomen or working on nerve centres along the spine to help relieve blockages, relieve congested tissue and improve the health of the body's organs.

complementary therapies

tips on using complementary therapies

→ Your doctor, health-food shop or friends may be able to suggest suitable practitioners.

→ Opt for gentle therapies. Avoid anything which is invasive, or involves harsh manipulation or fasting, which could be dangerous if you have a heart condition.

→ Make an appointment to discuss your condition and how the practitioner may be able to help. Check his or her training, qualifications and experience in treating people with your condition.

→ Check how many sessions the practitioner thinks you may need before you begin to feel any improvement and if there is none after this time, you will need to consider whether to carry on.

→ Avoid any therapist who suggests you stop taking your orthodox medicines. Let your doctor know of any complementary treatment you have been prescribed. Any changes in medication should only be carried out with his or her supervision.

REFLEXOLOGY

Reflexology is a type of massage which involves the therapist applying pressure to particular points on the feet and hands (although usually the feet) to improve mental and physical health. According to reflexology theory, these points correspond to various tissues and organs, and stimulating them unblocks energy in that particular organ, encouraging the body to heal itself. So, for example, the soft fleshy balls of your feet reflect your lungs, chest and shoulders, including the heart.

When the reflexologist is working on your feet, any pain or tenderness is said to be a sign of blockage or imbalance in the corresponding organ or body part. This is often manifested by crystalline deposits beneath the skin which feel like grains of sugar. The reflexologist will pay particular attention to these areas.

The therapy can be tremendously relaxing and is a safe system for people of any age. It is especially helpful for stress-related conditions and is also said to help relieve high blood pressure.

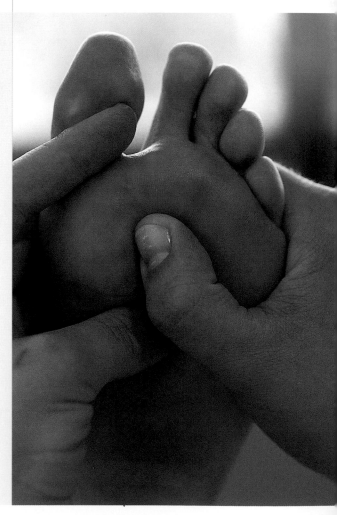

RIGHT: Reflexology is a relaxing therapy that can unblock energy and help relax both body and mind.

natural therapies

Natural therapies like homeopathy and Western herbalism are complete systems of therapy which aim to harness the body's own natural ability to heal itself to enhance health and cure disease.

RIGHT: A homeopathic consultation. The homeopath builds up a detailed picture of the individual and his symptoms before prescribing a remedy.

HOMEOPATHY

Homeopathy is a system of medicine devised in the 19th century by the German physician Samuel Hahnemann, although its origins are said to go even further back in history, to Hippocrates, the Ancient Greek father of medicine.

The theory behind homeopathy is the principle of similars or 'like treats like'. Unlike orthodox medicine, where drugs are given to counter symptoms, in homeopathy the remedies chosen are those which would provoke the symptoms of a particular illness in a healthy person. This is said to stimulate the body's own self-healing powers.

Another key principle is that of the minimum dose – that is, diluting an active ingredient over and over again actually increases its healing power, or potency. Thus homeopathic remedies are prepared by diluting a preparation of an active substance many times over and succussing, or shaking, it. The resulting drops are added to small milk-sugar tablets, pills, granules or powder. Homeopathic remedies are derived from plants, mineral salts or even poisons, but each ingredient is diluted so many times that it has no active pharmacological effect. Homeopaths believe that it is the energy, or 'vibrational pattern', of the remedy, not its chemical content, that stimulates the body's natural healing power.

The third key principle of homeopathy is whole-person prescribing. So the homeopath will ask a series of questions designed to find out what kind of person you are as well as your symptoms. He or she will then pick a remedy that matches the picture of you and your symptoms. For this reason, unlike in orthodox medicine where the same or similar drugs are used to treat particular conditions, in homeopathy two people with the same condition are unlikely to receive the same remedy.

Typical remedies used to treat angina, for example, may include: cactus, when the chest is constricted and there is difficulty breathing, cold sweat, pain down the left arm and low blood pressure; spigelia, where there is difficulty breathing which is relieved by lying on the right-hand side with head raised, palpitations and thirst for hot water; and naja, for when the pulse is irregular, stimulants make the condition worse and there is a feeling of weight on the heart, together with extreme anxiety and fear of death.

RIGHT: Many orthodox drugs used to treat heart disease were originally based on herbal remedies.

complementary therapies

WESTERN HERBALISM

Herbs and plants have been used down the ages to heal and cure illness. In fact, 80 per cent of the world's population still relies on herbal medicine, while many modern medicines were originally based on herbs. For example, aspirin, used to prevent heart attacks and strokes, was originally based on the white willow, while digitalis, used to treat heart disease, originally came from the foxglove.

Herbal remedies are prescribed to support your body as it attempts to heal itself – thus herbs are used not just to treat disease but to prevent recurrence and detoxify the system. Herbs can be administered in many different ways. They may be given as tinctures, infusions, decoctions, tablets and capsules, creams, ointments, hot or cold compresses, poultices, douches and herbal baths. Herbalists argue that herbal preparations are safer and gentler than modern pharmaceutical medicines because they use the whole plant, which often contains other ingredients which buffer or prevent harmful effects.

Nevertheless, the fact remains that herbs have a pharmacological action in the body – that is, like pharmaceutical drugs they change your body's chemistry. For this reason, apart from simple, mild herbal preparations like the teas you can buy in supermarkets, you should never mix herbal remedies with any drugs you have been prescribed by your doctor, unless both your doctor and the medical herbalist have advised it.

Having said that, herbs can have a definite place in the treatment of heart disease and its symptoms. For example, in one study carried out in 1993, garlic powder tablets were studied for their effects on blood fats, blood glucose and blood pressure in patients with raised cholesterol levels. The conclusion was that garlic significantly lowered levels of cholesterol compared with placebo.

LEFT: Garlic is especially beneficial for lowering cholesterol and boosting the health of the heart and blood vessels.

nutritional therapies

Therapies like naturopathy and nutritional therapy, which use food and diet to aid healing, can be some of the most useful in treating heart disease because of the known influence of food on factors such as blood pressure, weight and blood fat levels.

RIGHT: A number of nutritional supplements – vitamins, minerals and other natural chemicals found in food – may be recommended to keep the heart and blood vessels healthy.

NATUROPATHY

Naturopathy is a philosophy of life rather than a therapy as such. Naturopaths believe that simple basics – clean water, clean air, wholesome food, exercise and relaxation – are the foundations of a healthy lifestyle. Good health depends on maintaining a balance between the body's structure, its biochemistry and the emotions.

Naturopaths believe that the body naturally tends towards a state of harmony and health. Disease is seen as being a reflection of an imbalance brought about by poor diet, poor elimination of waste products, injury, inherited factors, destructive emotions or unhealthy living.

The symptoms of disease are seen as being the body's attempt to heal itself, and therefore naturopaths believe that they should not be suppressed but that the body should be supported as it recovers. This support may include diet, fasting, hydrotherapy, exercise, psychotherapy and manipulative techniques such as diet and massage.

Food and diet are the cornerstone of a naturopathic approach, and intriguingly the principles of a healthy diet laid down by naturopaths is very similar to that recommended by modern dietary experts for the prevention of heart disease. The naturopathic diet is virtually vegetarian and includes as many raw foods as possible. A small amount of protein, preferably derived from vegetables, unrefined carbohydrates and grains are included. Fasting is said to rest the digestive system, detoxify the body and stimulate the metabolism so healing can take place. However, fasting would not generally be recommended for people with serious illnesses, such as people with diabetes or heart disease.

NUTRITIONAL THERAPY

Nutritional therapy can include a number of different therapies, including macrobiotics, where a special diet, based around wholegrains and vegetables, is followed.

In a perfect world, it would be possible to get all the nutrients we need from a balanced diet. However, many nutritionists argue that because of intensive farming methods, and the use of pesticides, preservatives and additives, together with alcohol, smoking, stress and environmental pollution, food is not as nutritious as it could be and we are often short of nutrients. Many therefore believe that, in addition to eating a healthy diet rich in fruit and vegetables and low in animal fats, you should also take nutritional supplements to ensure that you get all the nutrients you need. Supplements that may be recommended for heart disease include fish oils, B vitamins, vitamin E and vitamin C. You will find more details about these in the next chapter.

Eating a healthy diet is one of the most important things you can do to prevent and treat heart disease. And the good news is that, unlike some conditions where the food connection is somewhat controversial, doctors and nutritional experts are in **virtually unanimous agreement on the kind of eating regimen they recommend for a healthy heart**. This consists of a diet rich in fruit and vegetables, fibre and unrefined carbohydrates, such as wholegrain cereals and root vegetables, and low in fatty foods.

Another piece of good news is that, unlike in the punitive days of the past when doctors stressed what kinds of food you must avoid, the emphasis nowadays is on the more positive aspects of food – that is, all the delicious foods you can eat for a healthy heart and blood vessels rather than what you cannot eat. This change of emphasis has very largely come about as a result of a number of exciting scientific discoveries made over the past decade or so, which have shown that **certain foods and nutrients can actively help to protect the heart and blood vessels** against disease.

the free radical connection

Free radicals, as you may remember from Chapter 1 of this book, are harmful molecules that damage the body's cells by causing oxidation, which is one of the key factors in the development of narrowed arteries.

Some people appear to be genetically predisposed to be more vulnerable to free-radical damage than others. However, the good news is that there are many foods that contain nutrients which actively help to protect against free-radical damage and prevent LDL cholesterol from being oxidized. Some of the most important of these are a group of nutrients known as antioxidants.

ANTIOXIDANT VITAMINS AND MINERALS

Antioxidants are nutrients that help to destroy free radicals and prevent the oxidation of LDL that wreaks such havoc in the blood vessels. Some of the most important antioxidants are the so-called ACE vitamins and minerals – that is, beta-carotene (which is converted into vitamin A in the body), vitamins C and E, and the mineral selenium, which is found in the soil. In fact, research has found that the use of antioxidants can decrease the rate of development of plaques in the arteries by half or more. Eating three antioxidant-rich fresh fruits either at mealtimes or as snacks, plus a substantial portion of vegetables and/or salad at least two of your main meals a day, will ensure that you get the minimum five fruit and vegetable portions a day needed for good health.

Other antioxidants include a group of nutrients called bioflavonoids, found in tea, red wine, apple skins and oranges, among many other foods. Alcohol dilates (opens) small blood vessels, thus increasing blood flow and also helps to increase levels of HDL (good) cholesterol. Unless you have liver or kidney problems, experts recommend drinking a glass of red wine a day to help reduce the risk of heart disease.

THE VITAL B VITAMINS

With the discovery that high levels of the amino acid homocysteine (if you remember from Chapter 2) may also be an important cause of oxidation of LDLs, scientists and nutritionists have been turning their attention to a new group of vitamins – folic acid (a type of B vitamin), vitamin B6 and vitamin B12 – as potential preventors of heart disease. Most people with high homocysteine levels have been found to have a low dietary intake of

BELOW: Doctors recommend a glass of red wine a day for cardiovascular health.

hese nutrients, which are thought to be necessary in the processing of homocysteine so that it does not build up in the blood. Replacing these vitamins can help to maintain normal homocysteine levels.

The panel on page 69 shows all the various nutrients that have been found to be beneficial for the heart and blood vessels, together with what they do and the best food sources for them. However, as a general rule of thumb, the best way to ensure that you get all the necessary nutrients is to eat a varied diet that contains plenty of fresh fruit and vegetables.

reducing levels of harmful blood fats

As well as making sure you get plenty of fresh fruit and vegetables, you also need to pay attention to maintaining a healthy level of fats in your diet. Three-quarters of the cholesterol in our bodies is made in the liver, but the remaining quarter is derived from the food we eat. In particular, eating too many saturated fats – that is, hard fats found mainly in animal products such as red meat, butter and hard or full-fat cheeses – can raise your cholesterol to unhealthy levels. Experts recommend that a third or less of our total fat intake should come from saturated fats.

As well as reducing the intake of animal fats, scientists say that we should also be reducing the amount of a group of fats known as trans-fats, which are found in processed foods such as many margarines, biscuits, cakes and pies as a result of a manufacturing process known as hydrogenation, used to solidify fats and oils. In fact, some experts argue that trans-fats are as harmful to the arteries as saturated fats.

increasing your intake of good fats

The good news is that not all fats are off the menu. Some fats are actually good for you, in that they actively protect the arteries against atherosclerosis by raising levels of 'good' HDL cholesterol, which helps to sweep away 'bad cholesterol', and having other beneficial effects on the arteries.

TOP: Lemons are a very good source of vitamin C, one of the antioxidant vitamins.

ABOVE: Fresh vegetables are a rich source of many of the nutrients that can help combat heart disease.

BELOW: Olives are one of the key ingredients in the Mediterranean diet that are thought to protect against heart disease.

BOTTOM: Sardines and other oily fish are rich in cardioprotective omega-3 fatty acids.

FAR RIGHT: Starchy foods, like these sweet potatoes, should form the basis of a healthy diet. They are also rich in beta-carotene, an antioxidant.

One of the most important groups of fats are omega-3 fatty acids, found particularly in oily fish such as herrings, mackerel, sardines, tuna, salmon and swordfish. The discovery of the benefits of omega-3 fatty acids came about as a result of studies of Greenland Eskimos (the Inuit people) who, although they have one of the fattiest diets in the world, have one of the lowest incidences of heart disease. It seems that their high intake of omega-3 fatty acids from seal and whale meat helps to protects them from atherosclerosis even though their diets are high in cholesterol. Non-fish sources of omega-3 fatty acids include soya beans and walnuts.

In trials, omega-3 fatty acids help to reduce high blood pressure and lower levels of cholesterol and to prevent clotting, as well as having an anti-inflammatory effect in people with raised blood pressure and high cholesterol levels. Another study showed that consuming the equivalent of one oily fish meal a week cut the risk of dying from sudden death due to heart disease by half. To gain maximum benefit, you should try to eat oily fish twice or three times a week.

Another group of beneficial fats are the omega-6 fatty acids found mainly in seeds and seed oils, such as hemp, flax, evening primrose and borage oil.

Olive oil is another source of omega-6 and also contains a fatty acid known as oleic acid, which has been found in some studies to help protect the arteries against atherosclerosis. It is thought that this may be one reason why people living in Mediterranean countries have lower levels of heart disease. Other sources include almonds and walnuts. Another important omega-6 fatty acid is linoleic acid which is found in vegetables and grains.

Other foods that can help enhance your blood-fat profile are garlic and onions, which contain compounds that help to lower blood pressure and levels of harmful LDL cholesterol and raise levels of beneficial HDL cholesterol in the blood.

the fibre factor

Many studies have shown that a high intake of fibre can help to lower cholesterol levels. The kind of fibre that is thought to be the most helpful is known as soluble fibre, a gluey substance found in lentils, kidney beans and other pulses, apples, pears, strawberries and blackberries, and cereals such as rye, barley, rice and oats, wholegrain bread and pasta. Starchy vegetables, such as potatoes, peas, squash, corn, yams and sweet potatoes, are other good sources.

Fibre may help in two ways: firstly, by producing substances in the body which inhibit the synthesis of LDL cholesterol; and, secondly, by buffering the effects of fat on the blood vessels so that less fat is absorbed and more is excreted.

As well as your daily five portions of fruit and vegetables, for maximum benefit you should aim to consume six portions a day of breads, cereals, including pasta (try to choose wholegrain varieties), and starchy vegetables.

NUTRIENTS FOR A HEALTHY HEART

NUTRIENT	FOUND IN	HOW CAN IT HELP
Beta-carotene	Carrots, apricots, peppers, asparagus, kale, spinach, cress, sweet potatoes, parsley, apples, garlic, ginger, papaya, rye	One of the ACE vitamins, it is converted into vitamin A in the body. Beta-carotene is an antioxidant that helps to reduce the harmful effects of free radicals. Beta-carotene supplements are, however, no longer recommended, especially in people who smoke, as they may accelerate the growth of lung cancer cells.
Vitamin C	Citrus fruit, watercress, garlic, onions, turnips, cayenne, sweet red pepper, parsley, walnuts, lemons, green leafy vegetables	Another of the antioxidant vitamins that helps to block oxidation of 'bad' LDL cholesterol.
Vitamin E	Apples, parsley, rye, wheatgerm, wholewheat, broccoli, eggs, alfalfa, nuts and seeds	The third key antioxidant. It is also an anticoagulant. In studies, it has been found to reduce the risk of heart attacks. Vitamin E is protected in the body by vitamin C, so the two should always be taken together.
Selenium	Wheatgerm, bran, onions, broccoli, tomatoes, shellfish, tuna	An antioxidant mineral that helps to protect against oxidative damage in the cells and ageing of many of the cells and tissues.
Bioflavonoids	Vegetable and fruit skins and leaves, including apples, grapes and oranges, and present in drinks made from them, such as tea and wine	Acts as an antioxidant to protect against the harmful effects of free radicals in the narrowing of the arteries.
Vitamin B6	Fish, egg yolk, wholegrain cereals, bananas, avocados, nuts, seeds, some green leafy vegetables	Works with vitamin B12 and folic acid to help lower levels of homocysteine.
Vitamin B12	Rye, sprouted seeds, pulses, eggs, kidney, liver, milk	Works with vitamin B6 and folic acid to help lower homocysteine levels.
Folic acid	Liver, kidneys, green leafy vegetables, fortified cereals, eggs	Works with vitamins B6 and B12 to reduce homocysteine levels.
Omega-3 fatty acids	Salmon, tuna, herring, mackerel, sardines, swordfish	Reduces levels of 'bad' LDL cholesterol, boosts levels of 'good' HDL cholesterol, helps prevent clotting.
Omega-6 fatty acids	Almonds, walnuts, vegetables, seeds and seed oils, grains	Helps protect against atherosclerosis.

supplementary benefits

Ideally, we should get all the nutrients we need from eating a well-balanced healthy diet, but certain supplements may help to protect against heart disease. For example, some studies show that supplements of vitamin E help to protect against atherosclerosis. Others show that vitamin C is beneficial, too. One point to bear in mind is that nutrients work synergistically – that is, in harmony with each other. For example, vitamin C protects vitamin E (an oily vitamin) from oxidation, while folic acid works best when combined with vitamins B6 and B12. The best way to get all the vitamins and minerals you need, therefore, is still to eat a varied diet. However, if you think you could benefit from a supplement it may be worth seeking the advice of your doctor or a nutritional practitioner or looking in the health-food shop for one that is specially designed for heart health.

cutting down on salt

Although we need some salt in our diets to maintain our body's sodium balance, a high intake of salt is linked to high blood pressure, one of the main risk factors for heart disease.

You can reduce your salt intake quite simply by limiting your consumption of processed and snack foods, which are generally high in salt to give them flavour, and foods such as bacon and salami, which are cured with salt, and by avoiding adding extra salt to your food at the table. Eating more fruit and vegetables, which naturally help to balance sodium levels because they contain potassium, is another positive step you can take.

maintaining a healthy weight

As we have already seen, one of the key risk factors for heart disease, and for other risk factors such as diabetes and high blood pressure, is being overweight. It can also worsen symptoms such as angina and shortness of breath by increasing the workload on your heart and lungs.

There are huge numbers of diets around, but the only real way to lose weight and to keep it off is to consume fewer calories than your body burns up and to burn more calories by becoming more active. Both of these parts of the equation are important in losing weight, but in terms of long-term weight control exercise is of paramount importance for the simple reason that, as we saw in Chapter 2, muscle is metabolically more active than fat. This means that your body continues burning calories even when you are at rest. Steer clear of very low-calorie diets and fad diets such as those which encourage you to eat a lot of fatty and protein foods. Experts agree that the best diet for both weight loss and overall health is built around starchy carbohydrates to provide fuel, together with fresh fruit, vegetables, salads and pulses, and a little lean meat, poultry and fish. You should limit your intake of fats of all kinds and of alcohol, which is high in 'empty' calories. Also avoid full-fat dairy products, fatty and sugary foods (like cakes, biscuits, sweets and snacks), and high-fat meat (such as sausages, bacon and fatty cuts like breast of lamb).

Changes in eating habits are more sustainable if you make them gradually and are realistic. You can help yourself to make healthier food choices by getting used to reading food labels and avoiding foods that are high in fat and sugar. By and large, processed foods are more likely to be high in fat and sugar, while simple, freshly cooked foods are likely to be low in these and high in beneficial vitamins, minerals and other nutrients. You can also reduce your calorie intake by substituting healthier foods for less healthy ones. So, for example, choose a bagel instead of a high-fat croissant for breakfast, a biscotto (a type of Italian biscuit) instead of a Danish pastry at coffee time, a pizza with a vegetable topping instead of a high-fat one loaded with salami and mozzarella, bread sticks instead of garlic bread, a baked potato instead of fries, a baked apple instead of apple pie.

BELOW LEFT: Get to know your local market and stock up on plenty of fresh fruit and vegetables.

BELOW: Green, leafy vegetables, like kale, are rich in folic acid which helps lower homocysteine levels.

different cuisines and heart disease

These days we are lucky enough to have the choice of the world's cuisines in recipe books, on supermarket shelves and in chill cabinets, and in ethnic restaurants, so it is helpful to know which ones are considered to be healthiest in terms of protecting against heart disease.

One of the protective factors in Japanese cuisine is one of the healthiest in the world, containing just over 30 per cent fat compared with 40 per cent in the United Kingdom. Not surprisingly, the Japanese have one of the world's lowest rates of heart disease.

One of the protective factors in Japanese cuisine is almost certainly its high levels of seafood and fish, including sushi. Other features of the Japanese diet include rice, soya bean products such as miso and tofu, various greens including seaweed, chicken and a variety of noodles. Cooking methods such as steaming and stir-frying, which use little fat, add to the health benefits of the Japanese diet. Beware of the high salt content of products such as soy sauce, however.

The Mediterranean diet has also come under a lot of scrutiny in recent years, due to the fact that people eating a traditional diet in regions such as Crete, southern Spain, Italy and the south of France have lower

BELOW: Oriental cuisine is extremely healthy both in terms of the foods consumed and low-fat cooking techniques such as stir-frying and steaming.

BELOW RIGHT: The Mediterranean diet and lifestyle is one of the best in the world for a healthy heart.

evels of heart disease than those living in northern European countries such as the United Kingdom, Scandinavia, Germany and the Netherlands.

Although it is relatively high in fat, the fat in the Mediterranean diet derives mainly from unsaturated fats found in olive oil, nuts and oily fish. Other features of the traditional Mediterranean diet include lots of green vegetables and herbs, wholegrain cereals, plenty of fruit and a small amount of meat, often game which is low in saturated fat, together with a moderate consumption of wine with meals. Just the kind of diet, in fact, that is recognized to help protect against atherosclerosis. Other beneficial factors in the traditional Mediterranean way of life include a high level of exercise and extended social support systems, which may help to reduce stress. Even though olive oil is less harmful in terms of your cholesterol levels than saturated fats, it is still important when choosing Mediterranean-inspired meals to go for ones that are low in fat to avoid becoming overweight.

Indian cuisine is one of the most varied in the world and is generally high in fresh vegetables, herbs, spices, onions and garlic, which can help to protect the heart. However, much of the Indian cuisine on offer in restaurants is high in meat and fats. If eating out in an Indian restaurant or buying Indian ready-meals, seek out vegetable dishes, such as the many vegetable curries available, dhal and dishes that are baked in the oven (such as many tandoori dishes) rather than those which come with rich creamy sauces, and go for boiled or steamed rice rather than pilau, which is often high in fat. If you are cooking Indian food at home, try to get hold of one of the increasing number of healthy Indian cookbooks now coming on the market or to adapt recipes so that they use less fat. It is usually possible to do this without sacrificing flavour.

Traditional African and African-Caribbean cuisine is extremely healthy, consisting as it does of various porridge or polenta-like dishes made from pounded maize or yam, rice and starchy vegetables, such as squashes, plantain, yams and sweet potatoes, and dishes such as jerk fish and chicken. However, some of the dishes on offer in African or Caribbean restaurants or take-aways are rather fatty and salty – try to choose simply prepared dishes rather than fatty meaty ones. If cooking at home, adapt your cooking methods to use less fat and salt.

eating for a healthy heart

→ Increase your intake of fresh fruit and vegetables, which are rich in antioxidant vitamins and minerals. Aim to consume at least five portions a day.

→ Base your diet around starchy, carbohydrate foods such as cereals and starchy vegetables like yams, potatoes, sweet potatoes and squash. These are good sources of fibre. Aim to consume six portions a day.

→ Be sparing with protein. Cut down on animal protein and eat more vegetable proteins. Aim for no more than two servings of lean protein a day.

→ Cut down your intake of red meat and high-fat animal products such as cheese, and increase your intake of foods containing healthy fats such as oily fish, seeds, nuts and their oils.

→ Save fatty, sugary foods such as pies, pastries, cakes and biscuits for the occasional treat.

→ Pay attention to cooking methods – grill, steam, bake and stir-fry using a very small amount of oil instead of frying, roasting and casseroling in rich creamy sauces.

→ Use herbs rather than butter to add interest to vegetables – for example, steam green beans with dill, potatoes with mint, courgettes with tarragon.

→ Sweeten dishes with apple juice or puréed pears and add spices such as cinnamon to give a hint of sweetness rather than using sugar.

→ Look for low-fat versions of cheeses, yogurt and dairy products.

→ Cut down on salt and use herbs, spices, garlic, onions, citrus juices and vinegars to add flavour instead.

chapter 7

This section contains a selection of recipes specifically designed to help keep your heart and blood vessels in good shape. Of course, we should all aim to eat a nutritious diet, but **it is especially important to be aware of what you eat if you have cardiovascular disease since your diet can prevent your condition from deteriorating and may even improve the health of your heart and blood vessels.**

The recipes that follow have been chosen from all around the world, with a particular emphasis on the cuisines of the Mediterranean and the Orient, which have been shown to be especially beneficial for the heart and blood vessels. You will find ideas for soups, starters, main courses – and a few puddings – based around healthy ingredients such as fruit and vegetables, pasta, rice, couscous and other grains, oily fish, game, nuts, seeds, herbs and olive oil. Each recipe is accompanied by an analysis showing the number of calories/kilojoules, grams of protein, carbohydrate, fat, saturated fat and fibre, to encourage you to make healthy choices.

black bean soup with soba noodles

Serves 4 – Preparation time: 10 minutes – Cooking time: 12 minutes

Per serving – 379 kcals/1594 kJ · Protein 14 g · Carbohydrate 48 g · Fat 16 g · Saturated fat 2 g · Fibre 7 g

200 g	**(7 oz) dried soba noodles**
2	**tablespoons groundnut or vegetable oil**
1	**bunch of spring onions, sliced**
2	**garlic cloves, roughly chopped**
1	**red chilli, deseeded and sliced**
4 cm	**(1½ inch) piece of fresh root ginger, peeled and grated**
125 ml	**(4 fl oz) black bean sauce or black bean stir-fry sauce**
750 ml	**(1¼ pints) vegetable stock**
200 g	**(7 oz) pak choi or spring greens, shredded**
2	**teaspoons soy sauce**
1	**teaspoon caster sugar**
50 g	**(2 oz) raw, unsalted shelled peanuts**

1 Cook the noodles in plenty of boiling water for about 5 minutes until just tender.

2 Meanwhile, heat the oil in a saucepan. Add the spring onions and garlic and fry gently for 1 minute.

3 Add the chilli, ginger, black bean sauce and stock and bring to the boil. Stir in the pak choi or spring greens, soy sauce, sugar and peanuts, reduce the heat and simmer gently, uncovered, for 4 minutes.

4 Drain the noodles and pile into serving bowls. Ladle over the soup and serve immediately.

thai seafood soup

Serves 4 – Preparation time: 20 minutes – Cooking time: 10 minutes

Per serving – 144 kcals/607 kJ · Protein 25 g · Carbohydrate 3 g · Fat 4 g · Saturated fat 0 g · Fibre 0 g

4   **kaffir lime leaves, or ¼ teaspoon grated lime rind**

nl   **(1¼ pints) chicken or fish stock**

1   **tablespoon Thai red curry paste**

1   **teaspoon salt**

2   **tablespoons Thai fish sauce**

4   **lemon grass stalks, finely chopped**

5   **galangal or ginger slices, finely chopped**

g   **(4 oz) cod fillet**

g   **(4 oz) raw prawns, shelled and deveined**

g   **(4 oz) crab claws**

g   **(4 oz) prepared squid, cut into bite-sized pieces**

g   **(4 oz) cooked mussels, shelled and debearded**

4   **Thai chillies, crushed**

2   **tablespoons lemon juice**

To Garnish:

    mint sprigs

1   **tablespoon chopped coriander leaves**

1   Remove the central ribs from the lime leaves, if using, dividing the leaves in half. Set aside.

2   Mix 2 tablespoons of the stock with the curry paste in a small saucepan. Heat the mixture, stirring, until it forms a sauce. Keep the sauce warm until required.

3   Bring the remaining stock to the boil in a large saucepan. Stir in the salt, fish sauce, lemon grass, lime leaves or grated lime rind and galangal or ginger.

4   Add the fish and seafood to the stock, return to the boil, then lower the heat and simmer gently for 5 minutes. Stir in the curry sauce, chillies and lemon juice, then transfer the soup to serving bowls. Garnish with mint sprigs and chopped coriander and serve immediately.

minestrone soup

Serves 4 – Preparation time: 10–15 minutes – Cooking time: 25 minutes

Per serving – 236 kcals/990 kJ · Protein 11 g · Carbohydrate 26 g · Fat 11 g · Saturated fat 3 g · Fibre 6 g

2   **tablespoons olive oil**

1   **onion, diced**

1   **garlic clove, crushed**

2   **celery sticks, chopped**

1   **leek, finely sliced**

1   **carrot, chopped**

400 g   **(13 oz) can chopped tomatoes**

600 ml   **(1 pint) chicken or vegetable stock**

1   **courgette, diced**

½   **small cabbage, shredded**

1   **bay leaf**

75 g   **(3 oz) canned haricot beans, drained**

75 g   **(3 oz) dried spaghetti, broken into small pieces, or small pasta shapes**

1   **tablespoon chopped flat leaf parsley**
    salt
    pepper

50 g   **(2 oz) Parmesan cheese, freshly grated, to serve**

1   Heat the oil in a large saucepan. Add the onion, garlic, celery, leek and carrot and sauté over a medium heat, stirring occasionally, for 3 minutes.

2   Add the tomatoes, stock, courgette, cabbage, bay leaf and haricot beans. Bring to the boil, lower the heat and simmer for 10 minutes.

3   Add the pasta and season to taste with salt and pepper. Stir well and cook for a further 8 minutes. Keep stirring as the soup may stick to the base of the pan.

4   Just before serving, add the chopped parsley and stir well. Ladle into warm soup bowls and serve with grated Parmesan.

sicilian fish soup

Serves 6 – Preparation time: 30 minutes – Cooking time: 45 minutes

Per serving – 595 kcals/2490 kJ · Protein 72 g · Carbohydrate 8 g · Fat 27 g · Saturated fat 4 g · Fibre 3 g

1 kg	(2 lb) fresh mussels and clams, scrubbed and debearded
500 g	(1 lb) small squid, cleaned and sliced
500 g	(1 lb) raw prawns, peeled
1.75 kg	(3½ lb) whole mixed fish (not oily fish) chopped parsley, to garnish

Broth:

150 ml	(¼ pint) extra virgin olive oil
4	leeks, sliced
4	garlic cloves, finely chopped
300 ml	(½ pint) dry white wine
	large pinch of saffron threads
750 g	(1½ lb) ripe plum tomatoes, roughly chopped
2	tablespoons sun-dried tomato purée or 6 sun-dried tomato pieces in oil, drained and roughly chopped
1	teaspoon fennel seeds
1	tablespoon dried oregano
600 ml	(1 pint) water
	salt
	pepper

1 First make the broth. Heat the olive oil in a large, flame-proof earthenware casserole, add the leeks and garlic and cook gently for about 5 minutes until the leeks are softening. Pour in the white wine and boil rapidly until reduced by half, then add the saffron, tomatoes, sun-dried tomato purée or sun-dried tomatoes, fennel seeds and dried oregano. Pour in the water and bring to the boil. Reduce the heat, cover the casserole and simmer for 20 minutes until the tomatoes and oil separate.

2 Place the mussels and clams in a bowl of cold water.

3 Cook the seafood as follows. Add the squid to the casserole and poach for 3–4 minutes. Remove with a slotted spoon, cover and keep warm. Add the prawns and simmer until opaque and cooked. Remove with a slotted spoon and keep warm with the squid. Drain the mussels and clams and add to the broth, cover and boil for a few minutes until they open. Remove with a slotted spoon and keep warm, discarding any that have not opened. Poach all the remaining fish in the broth until just cooked then remove them.

4 To serve, arrange all the fish on a serving dish with the mussels and clams, squid and prawns on top. Taste and season the broth. Moisten the fish with some of the broth and serve the rest of the broth separately. Garnish with chopped parsley.

hot and sour soup

Serves 6 – Preparation time: 10 minutes, plus soaking – Cooking time: about 15 minutes
Per serving – 63 kcals/266 kJ · Protein 7 g · Carbohydrate 5 g · Fat 2 g · Saturated fat 1 g · Fibre 0 g

15 g	(½ oz) dried shiitake mushrooms
25 ml	(4 fl oz) hot water
150 g	(5 oz) boneless cooked chicken, shredded
litre	(1¾ pints) chicken stock
2	tablespoons rice wine vinegar, white wine vinegar or cider vinegar
2	tablespoons light soy sauce
1	teaspoon sugar
1	red chilli, deseeded and very finely sliced
4	spring onions, very finely sliced on the diagonal
2	teaspoons cornflour

1 Soak the dried mushrooms in the hot water for 35–40 minutes. Drain the mushrooms into a sieve over a bowl and reserve the soaking water. Finely slice the mushrooms, discarding any hard stalks.

2 Bring the stock to the boil in a large saucepan. Add the vinegar and soy sauce, then the sugar, mushrooms and strained soaking water. Simmer for 5 minutes. Add half the chilli and spring onions, stir well and simmer for 5 minutes more. Add the chicken, stir and cook for 1–2 minutes. Blend the cornflour to a paste with a little cold water, then pour it into the soup and stir to mix. Simmer, stirring, for 1–2 minutes until the soup thickens.

3 Taste and add more vinegar and soy sauce, if necessary. Sprinkle with the remaining chilli and spring onions.

eight treasure soup

Serves 6 – Preparation time: 15–20 minutes – Cooking time: about 15 minutes
Per serving – 149 kcals/627 kJ · Protein 17 g · Carbohydrate 13 g · Fat 4 g · Saturated fat 1 g · Fibre 2 g

1.2	litres (2 pints) chicken stock or water
50 g	(2 oz) frozen peas
50 g	(2 oz) frozen sweetcorn kernels
1	small boneless, skinless chicken breast, cut into very thin strips
75 g	(3 oz) fresh shiitake mushrooms, thinly sliced with stalks removed
3	tablespoons soy sauce
2	tablespoons Chinese rice wine or dry sherry
1	tablespoon cornflour
50 g	(2 oz) cooked peeled prawns
50 g	(2 oz) cooked ham, thinly sliced
150 g	(5 oz) firm bean curd (tofu), drained and thinly sliced
50 g	(2 oz) baby spinach, very finely shredded
	salt
	pepper

1 Bring the stock or water to the boil in a large saucepan. Add the peas and sweetcorn and simmer for 3 minutes. Add the chicken, mushrooms, soy sauce and rice wine or sherry. Stir well and simmer for 3 minutes.

2 Blend the cornflour to a paste with a little cold water, then pour it into the soup and stir to mix. Simmer, stirring, for 1–2 minutes until the soup thickens.

3 Turn the heat down to low and add the prawns, ham, bean curd and spinach. Simmer for about 2 minutes until the spinach is just wilted, stirring once or twice. Take care to stir gently so that the bean curd does not break up. Taste and add salt and pepper, plus more soy sauce if you like. Serve piping hot.

tomato and bread soup

Serves 4 – Preparation time: 15 minutes – Cooking time: 40 minutes

Per serving – 250 kcals /1050 kJ · Protein 4 g · Carbohydrate 20 g · Fat 18 g · Saturated fat 3 g · Fibre 4 g

1 kg	**(2 lb) really ripe tomatoes, skinned, deseeded and chopped**
300 ml	**(½ pint) vegetable stock**
6	**tablespoons extra virgin olive oil**
2	**garlic cloves, crushed**
1	**teaspoon sugar**
2	**tablespoons chopped basil**
100 g	**(3½ oz) day-old bread without crusts**
1	**tablespoon balsamic vinegar**
	salt
	pepper

1 Place the tomatoes in a saucepan with the stock, 2 tablespoons of the oil, the garlic, sugar and basil and bring gradually to the boil. Cover the pan and simmer gently for 30 minutes.

2 Crumble the bread into the soup and stir over a low heat until it has thickened. Stir in the vinegar and the remaining oil and season with salt and pepper to taste. Serve immediately or leave to cool to room temperature

aubergine pâté

Serves 6 – Preparation time: 10 minutes – Cooking time: 15 minutes

Per serving – 157 kcals/650 kJ · Protein 3 g · Carbohydrate 6 g · Fat 14 g · Saturated fat 2 g · Fibre 3 g

25 g	**(1 oz) dried porcini mushrooms**
6	**tablespoons olive oil**
500 g	**(1 lb) aubergines, diced**
1	**small red onion, chopped**
2	**teaspoons cumin seeds**
175 g	**(6 oz) button or chestnut mushrooms**
2	**garlic cloves, crushed**
3	**pickled walnuts, halved**
	small handful of coriander leaves
	salt
	pepper
	toasted walnut or grainy bread, to serve

1 Place the dried mushrooms in a bowl and cover with plenty of boiling water. Leave to soak for 10 minutes.

2 Meanwhile, heat the oil in a large frying pan. Add the aubergines and onion and fry gently for 8 minutes until the vegetables are softened and browned.

3 Drain the dried mushrooms and add to the pan with the cumin seeds, fresh mushrooms and garlic. Fry for a further 5–7 minutes until the aubergines are very soft.

4 Transfer to a food processor or blender with the pickled walnuts and coriander, season to taste with salt and pepper and process until broken up but not completely smooth. Transfer to a serving dish and serve warm or cold with toast.

vietnamese salad rolls with dipping sauce

Serves 4 – Preparation time: 25 minutes

Per serving – 80 kcals/340 kJ · Protein 2 g · Carbohydrate 16 g · Fat 1 g · Saturated fat 0 g · Fibre 2 g

12 small rice paper spring roll wrappers
1 carrot, cut into fine matchsticks
1 cucumber, halved lengthways, deseeded and cut into fine matchsticks
125 g (4 oz) enoki mushrooms or bean sprouts
2 spring onions, finely shredded
15 g (½ oz) mint leaves
15 g (½ oz) coriander leaves

Dipping Sauce:
2 tablespoons Vietnamese fish sauce
3 tablespoons lime juice
2 teaspoons caster sugar
1 small red chilli, deseeded and finely sliced

1 Soak the spring roll wrappers in hot water for 1–2 minutes or until softened, then drain well and lay the wrappers on a work surface or board and cover with a damp tea towel.

2 Divide the carrot, cucumber, enoki mushrooms or bean sprouts, spring onions, mint and coriander evenly between the wrappers. Fold and roll the wrappers around the salad filling to enclose it in neat packages. Place on a board and cover with a damp tea towel until ready to serve.

3 Mix all the ingredients for the dipping sauce and pour it into a small bowl. Arrange the salad rolls on a large platter or individual plates and serve with the dipping sauce.

SALADS

strawberry and cucumber salad with a balsamic dressing

Serves 4 – Preparation time: 15 minutes, plus chilling

Per serving – 108 kcals/447 kJ · Protein 1 g · Carbohydrate 7 g · Fat 9 g · Saturated fat 1 g · Fibre 2 g

1	**large cucumber, halved lengthways, deseeded and thinly sliced**
250 g	**(8 oz) strawberries, halved or quartered**

Balsamic Dressing:

1	**tablespoon balsamic vinegar**
1	**teaspoon coarse-grain mustard**
1	**teaspoon clear honey**
3	**tablespoons olive oil**
	salt
	pepper

1 Place the cucumber and strawberries in a shallow bowl.

2 To make the dressing, put all the ingredients in a screw-top jar and shake well.

3 Taste the dressing for seasoning and adjust if necessary then pour it over the cucumber and strawberries. Toss lightly and chill for 5–10 minutes before serving.

stir-fried noodles with broccoli, sweetcorn, bean sprouts and smoked tofu

Serves 4 – Preparation time: 20 minutes – Cooking time: 20 minutes

Per serving – 435 kcals/1825 kJ · Protein 23 g · Carbohydrate 47 g · Fat 18 g · Saturated fat 5 g · Fibre 5 g

175 g	(6 oz) dried thread egg noodles
250 g	(8 oz) broccoli florets
	sunflower oil, for deep-frying
250 g	(8 oz) firm smoked tofu, cubed
1	onion, finely chopped
1	teaspoon grated fresh root ginger
2	garlic cloves, crushed
1	small red chilli, deseeded and finely sliced
175 g	(6 oz) baby sweetcorn, cut in half lengthways
175 g	(6 oz) bean sprouts
2	red chillies, deseeded and cut in half, to garnish

Sauce:

50 ml	(8 fl oz) teriyaki sauce
2	tablespoons sake (Japanese rice wine)
2	tablespoons lemon juice
2–3	teaspoons sweet chilli sauce
2	teaspoons brown sugar

1 Cook the noodles in a large saucepan of boiling water according to packet instructions until just tender. Drain and refresh under cold running water until very cold. Leave to drain. Blanch the broccoli in a large saucepan of boiling water for about 1 minute, drain and refresh under cold water. Drain again and pat dry with kitchen paper. Combine all the ingredients for the sauce in a bowl and mix well.

2 Heat about 5 cm (2 inches) of sunflower oil in a heavy-based frying pan or wok and fry the tofu cubes for 3–4 minutes until crisp and lightly golden. Drain on kitchen paper and keep warm. Remove all but a few tablespoons of the oil from the wok and fry the onion, ginger, garlic and chilli until soft but not brown.

3 Add the broccoli and stir-fry for 2–3 minutes. Add the sweetcorn and bean sprouts and stir-fry for about 3 minutes. Add the sauce, toss to combine, then add the noodles and the fried tofu. Cook for another minute until heated through. Serve garnished with chilli halves.

persian noodles

Serves 4 – Preparation time: 10 minutes – Cooking time: about 20 minutes

Per serving – 152 kcals/643 kJ · Protein 6 g · Carbohydrate 28 g · Fat 3 g · Saturated fat 0 g · Fibre 3 g

600 ml	(1 pint) chicken or vegetable stock
125 g	(4 oz) noodles
1	large aubergine, cubed
4	courgettes, sliced
1	teaspoon ground mace
	salt
	pepper
	flat leaf parsley, to garnish

1 Place the stock in a large saucepan and bring to the boil. Add the noodles and cook for 5 minutes, then add the aubergine, courgettes and mace. Season with salt and pepper to taste.

2 Reduce the heat and cook for a further 10–15 minutes, or until the noodles and vegetables are tender. Adjust the seasoning to taste, then drain and divide between 4 serving dishes. Serve immediately, garnished with flat leaf parsley.

mixed vegetable curry

Serves 4 – Preparation time: 15 minutes – Cooking time: 20–25 minutes

Per serving – 118 kcals/494 kJ · Protein 3 g · Carbohydrate 13 g · Fat 6 g · Saturated fat 1 g · Fibre 5 g

2	tablespoons vegetable oil
1	small onion, chopped, or 2 teaspoons cumin seeds
500 g	(I lb) mixed vegetables, such as potatoes, carrots, swede, peas, green beans or cauliflower, cut into bite-sized pieces
	about 1 teaspoon chilli powder
2	teaspoons ground coriander
½	teaspoon ground turmeric
2–3	tomatoes, skinned and chopped
	salt

1 Heat the oil in a heavy-based saucepan. Add the onion and fry over a medium heat, stirring occasionally, until light brown. Alternatively, fry the cumin seeds until they pop. Add the mixed vegetables and stir in the chilli powder, ground coriander, turmeric and salt to taste. Fry for 2–3 minutes.

2 Add the chopped tomatoes. Stir well and add a little water. Cover and cook gently for 10–12 minutes, until the vegetables are tender and the mixture is dry. For a moister curry, stir in 300 ml (½ pint) water, then cover and simmer for 5–6 minutes, until the vegetables are tender. Serve hot.

courgette and mixed leaf salad

Serves 6 – Preparation time: 15 minutes, plus standing

Per serving – 50 kcals/210 kJ · Protein 2 g · Carbohydrate 5 g · Fat 3 g · Saturated fat 0 g · Fibre 1 g

4	tablespoons low-fat French dressing
1	garlic clove, crushed
275 g	(9 oz) courgettes, thinly sliced
500 g	(1 lb) salad leaves
50 g	(2 oz) green or black olives, halved and pitted
1	tablespoon pine nuts
	salt
	pepper

1 Put the French dressing and garlic into a salad bowl. Add the sliced courgettes and toss well. Leave to stand for 30 minutes to allow the courgettes to absorb the flavour of the dressing.

2 Tear the salad leaves into manageable pieces and add to the courgettes and dressing with the olives and pine nuts. Season with salt and pepper to taste. Toss the salad thoroughly before serving.

vegetable rice pancakes with sesame and ginger sauce

Serves 4 – Preparation time: 15 minutes – Cooking time: 5 minutes

Per serving – 187 kcals/789 kJ · Protein 4 g · Carbohydrate 35 g · Fat 4 g · Saturated fat 0 g · Fibre 3 g

8	rice pancakes
2	carrots
100 g	(3½ oz) bean sprouts or mixed sprouting beans
	small handful of mint, roughly chopped
1	celery stick, thinly sliced
4	spring onions, thinly sliced on the diagonal
1	tablespoon soy sauce

Sauce:

1	garlic clove, roughly chopped
5 cm	(2 inch) piece of fresh root ginger, peeled and roughly chopped
3	tablespoons light muscovado sugar
4	teaspoons soy sauce
5	teaspoons wine or rice vinegar
2	tablespoons tomato purée
2	tablespoons sesame seeds, plus extra to garnish

1 Place all the ingredients for the sauce, except the sesame seeds, in a food processor or blender and process to a thin paste. Alternatively, crush the garlic, grate the ginger and whisk with the remaining ingredients. Stir in the sesame seeds and transfer to a serving bowl.

2 Soften the rice pancakes according to the packet instructions. Cut the carrots into fine sheds and mix with the bean sprouts or sprouting beans, mint, celery, spring onions and soy sauce.

3 Divide the vegetable mixture between the 8 pancakes and spoon into the middle of each. Fold the bottom edge of each pancake to the middle, then roll up from one side to the other to form a pocket.

4 Steam the pancakes in a vegetable steamer or bamboo steamer for about 5 minutes until heated through. Alternatively, place on a wire rack set over a roasting tin of boiling water and cover with foil. Serve immediately with the sauce, and garnished with sesame seeds.

baby squash with red bean sauce

Serves 4 – Preparation time: 10 minutes – Cooking time: 20 minutes

Per serving – 330 kcals/1387 kJ · Protein 12 g · Carbohydrate 45 g · Fat 13 g · Saturated fat 2 g · Fibre 10 g

600 ml	**(1 pint) vegetable stock**
1 kg	**(2 lb) mixed baby squash, such as gem, butternut or acorn**
125 g	**(4 oz) baby spinach**
	steamed rice, to serve
	Sauce:
4	**tablespoons olive oil**
4	**garlic cloves, thinly sliced**
1	**red pepper, cored, deseeded and finely chopped**
2	**tomatoes, chopped**
425 g	**(14 oz) can red kidney beans, rinsed and drained**
1–2	**tablespoons hot chilli sauce**
	small handful of chopped coriander
	salt

1 Bring the stock to the boil in a large saucepan. Quarter and deseed the squash. Add to the pan, reduce the heat and cover. Simmer gently for about 15 minutes or until just tender.

2 Meanwhile, to make the sauce, heat the oil in a frying pan, add the garlic and pepper and fry for 5 minutes, stirring frequently, until very soft. Add the tomatoes, red kidney beans, chilli sauce and a little salt and simmer for 5 minutes until pulpy.

3 Drain the squash from the stock, reserving the stock, and return to the rinsed pan. Scatter over the spinach leaves, cover the pan and cook for about 1 minute until the spinach has wilted.

4 Pile the vegetables on to warmed serving plates. Stir 8 tablespoons of the reserved stock into the sauce with the coriander. Spoon over the vegetables and serve hot, accompanied with steamed rice.

stir-fried bok-choy

Serves 3 – Preparation time: 10 minutes – Cooking time: about 5 minutes

Per serving – 96 kcals/397 kJ · Protein 2 g · Carbohydrate 5 g · Fat 8 g · Saturated fat 1 g · Fibre 2 g

375 g	**(12 oz) bok-choy**
2	**tablespoons groundnut oil**
2	**garlic cloves, finely chopped**
2	**teaspoons sugar**
2	**dried red chillies**
1	**tablespoon soy sauce**
1	**tablespoon rice wine vinegar,**
	white wine vinegar or cider vinegar
	salt
	sesame oil, for drizzling

1 Trim the white stalks off the bok-choy, then cut the stalks into 4 cm (1½ inch) lengths. Tear or roughly shred the green leaves.

2 Heat an empty wok until hot. Add the groundnut oil and heat until hot. Add the bok-choy stalks, garlic, sugar and salt to taste. Crumble the dried chillies over the bok-choy and stir-fry over a moderate to high heat for 2 minutes.

3 Add the bok-choy leaves, soy sauce and vinegar and toss vigorously for 30–60 seconds until the leaves start to wilt. Serve immediately, sprinkled with sesame oil.

sweet and sour courgettes and carrots

Serves 4 – Preparation time: 10 minutes, plus standing – Cooking time: 10 minutes

Per serving – 156 kcals/647 kJ · Protein 2 g · Carbohydrate 12 g · Fat 12 g · Saturated fat 2 g · Fibre 2 g

4	**tablespoons olive oil**
375 g	**(12 oz) courgettes, thinly sliced**
375 g	**(12 oz) carrots, thinly sliced**
2	**tablespoons white wine vinegar**
2	**tablespoons shredded mint**
1	**tablespoon salted capers, rinsed and**
	roughly chopped
	salt
	pepper
	mint sprigs, to garnish

1 Heat the oil in a frying pan and sauté the courgettes and carrots in batches until golden brown. As they are ready, remove them to a warmed serving dish with a slotted spoon, leaving any oil in the bottom of the pan. Season with salt and pepper.

2 Add the vinegar and mint to the pan and bring to the boil, then immediately pour this dressing over the vegetables and carefully toss to mix. Leave the dish to stand at room temperature for at least 30 minutes to allow the flavours to develop. To serve, scatter with the capers and garnish with mint sprigs.

peperonata

Serves 4 – Preparation time: 10 minutes – Cooking time: 1–1¼ hours

Per serving – 164 kcals/685 kJ · Protein 4 g · Carbohydrate 18 g · Fat 9 g · Saturated fat 1 g · Fibre 5 g

3	tablespoons olive oil
2	onions, sliced
3	garlic cloves, chopped
2	yellow peppers, cored, deseeded and cut into thick strips
2	red peppers, cored, deseeded and cut into thick strips
1 kg	(2 lb) ripe tomatoes, skinned, deseeded and chopped, or 2 x 400 g (13 oz) cans chopped tomatoes
	salt
	pepper

1 Heat the olive oil in a saucepan, add the onions and garlic and cook over a gentle heat for at least 20 minutes until golden and caramelized.

2 Add the yellow and red peppers to the onions, cover the pan and cook for 10 minutes to soften the peppers.

3 Stir the tomatoes into the pepper mixture and simmer uncovered for 30–45 minutes until soft, thick and reduced. Taste and season with salt and pepper. Serve warm or at room temperature.

braised baby artichokes and fresh peas with mint

Serves 6 – Preparation time: 30 minutes – Cooking time: 25 minutes

Per serving – 185 kcals/767 kJ · Protein 11 g · Carbohydrate 24 g · Fat 5 g · Saturated fat 1 g · Fibre 3 g

2	**tablespoons olive oil**
6	**spring onions, chopped**
1	**garlic clove, crushed**
12	**fresh baby artichokes**
	lemon juice, for brushing
75 ml	**(3 fl oz) water**
1 kg	**(2 lb) fresh peas, shelled**
2	**tablespoons chopped mixed mint and parsley**
	salt
	pepper
	mint sprigs, to garnish

1 Heat the oil in a casserole, add the spring onions and garlic and cook gently for 5 minutes until they begin to soften. Set aside.

2 Trim the artichoke stalks to about 1 cm (½ inch). Break off the tough outside leaves, starting at the base, until you expose a central core of pale leaves. Slice off the tough green or purple tips. With a small sharp knife, pare the dark green skin from the base and down the stem. Cut the artichokes in half and brush the cut sides with lemon juice to prevent them from browning.

3 Return the spring onions to the heat and add the artichokes and water. Cover the casserole tightly and simmer for 10 minutes or until the artichokes are almost tender. Gently stir in the peas, mint and parsley and a little extra water if necessary. Replace the lid and cook for a further 10 minutes. Season to taste and serve garnished with mint sprigs.

mediterranean kebabs

Serves 4 – Preparation time: 20 minutes – Cooking time: 6–8 minutes

Per serving – 98 kcals/406 kJ · Protein 2 g · Carbohydrate 9 g · Fat 6 g · Saturated fat 1 g · Fibre 2 g

2	courgettes
12	cherry tomatoes
1	red onion, cut into 8 wedges
1	red pepper, cored, deseeded and cut into squares
2	tablespoons olive oil
1	tablespoon finely chopped flat leaf parsley
½	teaspoon chilli flakes
4	tablespoons lemon juice
1	garlic clove, crushed
	salt
	pepper
	chopped thyme, to garnish

To Serve:
**steamed rice or a crisp green salad
lemon wedges**

1 Trim the courgettes, then use a vegetable peeler to cut them lengthways into very thin slices or ribbons. Place the courgettes in a shallow bowl and add the tomatoes, onion and red pepper.

2 Mix the oil, parsley, chilli flakes, lemon juice, garlic and salt and pepper. Pour this mixture over the vegetables and set them aside to marinate for at least 5 minutes.

3 Thread the vegetables on to 8 medium or 4 large metal skewers, making sure there is a variety of vegetables on each skewer and threading the strips of courgette between and around the other vegetables. Reserve the juices from the marinade.

4 Brush the vegetables with the reserved marinade. Cook the kebabs under a preheated grill heated to its hottest setting, turning them frequently, for about 6–8 minutes, until the vegetables are cooked. Garnish with thyme and serve with rice or a green salad and lemon wedges.

fresh vegetable pizza

Serves 4 – Preparation time: 30 minutes – Cooking time: 10 minutes

Per serving – 495 kcals/2078 kJ · Protein 19 g · Carbohydrate 60 g · Fat 22 g · Saturated fat 6 g · Fibre 7 g

250 g	(8 oz) self-raising flour
150 ml	(¼ pint) warm water
5	tablespoons olive oil
2	garlic cloves, chopped
1	red onion, finely sliced
2	courgettes, thinly sliced lengthways
1	red pepper, cored, deseeded and cut into thin strips
1	yellow pepper, cored, deseeded and cut into thin strips
4	plum tomatoes, skinned, cored and cut into small wedges
500 g	(I lb) asparagus, trimmed
4	thyme sprigs, separated into leaves
	handful of basil leaves, roughly torn
	salt
	pepper
75 g	(3 oz) Parmesan shavings, to serve

1 Place the flour and 1 teaspoon of salt in a large bowl and mix well. Slowly add the warm water and mix to a soft dough. Turn out the dough on to a lightly floured surface and knead until smooth and soft, then roll into a large rectangle.

2 Place the pizza base on a warmed baking sheet and brush with a little olive oil. Arrange the vegetables on the base, sprinkling them with the thyme leaves and roughly torn basil.

3 Season the pizza generously with salt and pepper, drizzle with more olive oil and bake at the top of a preheated oven at 230°C (450°F), Gas Mark 8 for 10 minutes. The vegetables should be slightly charred around the edges as this adds to the flavour. Serve with fresh Parmesan shavings.

clam, potato and bean stew

Serves 6 – Preparation time: 20 minutes – Cooking time: 40 minutes

Per serving – 379 kcals/1578 kJ · Protein 15 g · Carbohydrate 14 g · Fat 30 g · Saturated fat 6 g · Fibre 4 g

2	**tablespoons olive oil**
125 g	**(4 oz) piece of unsmoked pancetta, diced**
1	**onion, chopped**
375 g	**(12 oz) potatoes, cubed**
1	**leek, sliced**
2	**garlic cloves, crushed**
1	**tablespoon chopped rosemary**
2	**bay leaves**
400 g	**(13 oz) can cannellini beans, drained**
900 ml	**(1½ pints) vegetable stock**
1 kg	**(2 lb) small clams or mussels, scrubbed and debearded**
	salt
	pepper

Garlic and Parsley Oil:

150 ml	**(¼ pint) extra virgin olive oil**
2	**large garlic cloves, sliced**
¼	**teaspoon salt**
1	**tablespoon chopped parsley**

1 Heat the oil in a large saucepan and fry the pancetta for 5 minutes, until golden. Remove from the pan with a slotted spoon. Add the onion, potatoes, leek, garlic, rosemary and bay leaves to the pan and sauté gently for 10 minutes, until softened. Add the beans and stock, bring to the boil and simmer gently for 20 minutes, until the vegetables are tender.

2 Meanwhile, make the garlic and parsley oil. Heat the oil with the garlic and salt in a small pan and simmer gently for 3 minutes. Leave to cool, then stir in the parsley. Set aside.

3 Transfer half of the stew to a food processor or blender and blend until really smooth, then pour it back into the pan and season with salt and pepper to taste. Stir in the clams or mussels and add the pancetta. Simmer gently until the shellfish are open, about 5 minutes (discard any that remain closed). Spoon the stew into bowls and drizzle with the garlic and parsley oil.

hake with peppers

Serves 4 – Preparation time: 15 minutes – Cooking time: 45 minutes

Per serving – 410 kcals/1718 kJ · Protein 39 g · Carbohydrate 24 g · Fat 16 g · Saturated fat 2 g · Fibre 3 g

4	**tablespoons olive oil**
4	**small red peppers, cored, deseeded and thickly sliced**
4	**garlic cloves, peeled**
2	**thyme sprigs**
	pinch of hot paprika
75 ml	**(3 fl oz) dry sherry**
4	**potatoes**
4 x	**175 g (6 oz) hake steaks**
2	**bay leaves**
	salt
	pepper

To Serve:
crusty bread
aïoli or garlic mayonnaise

1 Heat the oil in a flameproof casserole, add the peppers, garlic, thyme sprigs and paprika and fry over a gentle heat for 15–20 minutes, stirring frequently, until browned and softened. Add the sherry and boil rapidly until reduced by half.

2 Meanwhile, parboil the potatoes for 10–12 minutes, until nearly cooked. Refresh under cold water and cut into cubes.

3 Stir the potatoes into the pepper mixture with some salt and pepper. Season the hake steaks and arrange them on top, pressing them down into the peppers slightly. Add the bay leaves and 4 tablespoons of water, cover the casserole and simmer gently over a low heat for 15–20 minutes, depending on the thickness of the fish. Leave the fish to rest for a few minutes then serve with crusty bread and aïoli or garlic mayonnaise.

mullet with vine leaves

Serves 4 – Preparation time: 30 minutes – Cooking time: 8–10 minutes

Per serving – 329 kcals/1373 kJ · Protein 30 g · Carbohydrate 1 g · Fat 23 g · Saturated fat 2 g · Fibre 1 g

6   **tablespoons olive oil**
2   **tablespoons lemon juice**
2   **tablespoons chopped dill**
2   **spring onions, chopped**
1   **teaspoon mustard powder**
8   **vine leaves in brine, drained**
4   **red mullet, scaled and gutted**
4   **bay leaves**
4   **dill sprigs**
    salt
    pepper
    tomato and olive salad, to serve
      (optional)

To Garnish:
lemon wedges
dill sprigs

1 Put four pieces of string, about 30 cm (12 inches) long into cold water to soak for 10 minutes.

2 In a bowl, combine the oil, lemon juice, chopped dill, spring onions, mustard powder and salt and pepper. Wash and dry the vine leaves and arrange them in pairs overlapping them slightly.

3 Make several slashes on both sides of each fish and rub them all over with a little of the oil and lemon mixture. Stuff each of the belly cavities with a bay leaf and a dill sprig. Wrap each fish in a couple of vine leaves, brush with a little oil and fasten with the wet string to secure the leaves in place.

4 Grill, griddle or barbecue the fish for 4–5 minutes on each side, brushing them with a little more oil if necessary, until lightly charred. Leave the fish to rest for a few minutes, then discard the vine leaves and dress the mullet with the rest of the lemon oil. Garnish with lemon wedges and dill sprigs and serve with a tomato and olive salad, if liked.

swordfish steaks with charmoula and pepper salsa

Serves 4 – Preparation time: 20 minutes, plus marinating – Cooking time: 20 minutes

Per serving – 254 kcals/1063 kJ · Protein 28 g · Carbohydrate 3 g · Fat 15 g · Saturated fat 3 g · Fibre 1 g

4 x   **150 g (5 oz) swordfish steaks**
      lime wedges, to garnish

Charmoula:

1   **teaspoon paprika**
½   **teaspoon ground turmeric**
½   **teaspoon ground cumin**
2   **garlic cloves, crushed**
2   **tablespoons chopped coriander**
1   **tablespoon lime juice**
2   **tablespoons olive oil**
     salt
     pepper

Pepper Salsa:

2   **red peppers, halved, cored and**
      deseeded
1   **small red chilli**
4   **spring onions, chopped**
½   **garlic clove, crushed**
4   **ripe tomatoes, skinned, deseeded**
      and diced
1   **tablespoon lemon juice**
1   **teaspoon olive oil**

1 Place the swordfish in a glass or ceramic dish. Combine all the charmoula ingredients, brush over both sides of the steaks, cover and marinate for at least 4 hours, preferably overnight.

2 To make the salsa, char the pepper halves, skin side up, and the chilli under a hot grill until blackened. Place in a plastic bag and leave to cool. When cool enough to handle, slip off the skins and chop the flesh. Toss in a small bowl with all the remaining salsa ingredients, season to taste with salt and pepper and set aside.

3 Cook the marinated swordfish steaks under a preheated moderately hot grill for 3–4 minutes on each side, basting them with any marinade left in the bowl, until the fish is charred and tender. Alternatively, cook over moderately hot coals on a barbecue.

4 Serve the swordfish at once with the grilled pepper salsa and garnished with lime wedges.

trout stuffed with couscous and herbs

Serves 4 – Preparation time: 10 minutes, plus standing – Cooking time: 25–30 minutes

Per serving – 434 kcals/1815 kJ · Protein 44 g · Carbohydrate 19 g · Fat 21 g · Saturated fat 3 g · Fibre 2 g

1	tablespoon olive oil
1	small onion, finely chopped
2	garlic cloves, crushed
125 g	(4 oz) couscous
300 ml	(½ pint) fish or vegetable stock
1	tablespoon chopped parsley
1	tablespoon chopped mint
4 x	300 g (10 oz) trout, gutted, heads removed, and boned
50 g	(2 oz) flaked almonds (optional)
	salt
	pepper

To Garnish:
lemon wedges
mint sprigs

1 Heat the oil in a frying pan, add the onion and fry until softened, adding the garlic towards the end. Stir in the couscous, stock, parsley and mint. Bring to the boil then remove the pan from the heat and leave for 10–15 minutes until the liquid has been absorbed.

2 Season the trout with salt and pepper and fill the cavity of each one with a quarter of the couscous mixture. Lay the fish in a lightly greased shallow baking dish and sprinkle over the almonds, if using. Bake in a preheated oven at 200°C (400°F), Gas Mark 6 for 15–20 minutes until the fish flakes easily.

3 Serve the trout garnished with lemon wedges and mint sprigs.

prawns in chilli tomato sauce

Serves 4 – Preparation time: 10 minutes – Cooking time: 10–12 minutes

Per serving – 225 kcals/944 kJ · Protein 30 g · Carbohydrate 9 g · Fat 8 g · Saturated fat 1 g · Fibre 2 g

2	tablespoons olive oil
2	red onions, finely chopped
3	garlic cloves, crushed
1	fresh red chilli, deseeded and chopped
2	strips of lemon rind
2	large, ripe, well-flavoured tomatoes, deseeded and chopped
150 ml	(¼ pint) fish stock
500 g	(1 lb) raw tiger prawns, peeled
	salt
	pepper
2	tablespoons chopped mixed parsley and dill, to garnish

1 Heat the oil in a heavy-based frying pan. Add the onions, garlic, chilli and lemon rind and fry over a medium heat, stirring occasionally, for 1–2 minutes. Add the tomatoes and fish stock and bring to the boil, then lower the heat and simmer for 5 minutes.

2 Add the prawns to the sauce, season to taste with salt and pepper and cook, turning occasionally, for about 4 minutes until the prawns change colour. Sprinkle with the mixed herbs and serve immediately.

fish plaki

Serves 4 – Preparation time: 10 minutes – Cooking time: 1 hour

Per serving – 353 kcals/1478 kJ · Protein 43 g · Carbohydrate 9 g · Fat 15 g · Saturated fat 2 g · Fibre 3 g

1.25 kg	(2½ lb) fish, such as a whole bass or grey mullet
1	large lemon
2	tablespoons virgin olive oil
1	onion, chopped
1	carrot, finely chopped
2	garlic cloves, chopped
1	teaspoon coriander seeds, crushed
500 g	(1 lb) ripe tomatoes, skinned, deseeded and chopped
3	sun-dried tomato pieces, chopped
75 ml	(3 fl oz) dry white wine
	bunch of parsley, finely chopped
	salt
	pepper
	parsley sprig, to garnish

1 Put the fish into an ovenproof dish. Squeeze the juice from half the lemon and pour it over the fish.

2 Heat the olive oil in a saucepan. Add the onion and carrot and cook, stirring occasionally, until the onion has softened but not coloured. Stir in the chopped garlic and cook for about 3 minutes.

3 Stir in the coriander seeds, tomatoes, sun-dried tomatoes, wine and parsley and season to taste with salt and pepper. Lower the heat and simmer for a few minutes, until well blended. Using a fish slice, lift the fish and pour about a quarter of the tomato mixture underneath. Pour the remaining tomato mixture over the fish. Thinly slice the remaining lemon half and lay the slices on top of the fish.

4 Cover the dish and bake in a preheated oven at 190°C (375°F), Gas Mark 5 for about 40 minutes until the fish flakes easily. Garnish with a parsley sprig and serve hot.

roast garlic-studded monkfish

Serves 4 – Preparation time: 20 minutes, plus marinating – Cooking time: about 30 minutes

Per serving – 260 kcals/1093 kJ · Protein 30 g · Carbohydrate 8 g · Fat 13 g · Saturated fat 2 g · Fibre 3 g

1 kg	**(2 lb) monkfish tail**
3–4	**bay leaves**
1	**teaspoon fennel seeds**
4–6	**garlic cloves, cut into thick slivers**
4	**tablespoons olive oil**
	a few thyme sprigs
2	**red peppers, halved, deseeded and roughly chopped**
1	**aubergine, cubed**
2	**courgettes, cubed**
3	**ripe plum tomatoes, cubed**
3	**tablespoons lemon juice**
	salt
	pepper

To Garnish:

2	**tablespoons salted capers, rinsed and chopped**
3	**tablespoons chopped parsley**

1 Trim any membrane and dark meat from the monkfish. Remove the central bone by slitting the fish down the middle until you reach the bone. Turn the fish over and do the same on the other side. Ease out the bone, gently scraping the flesh away with the tip of a knife.

2 Lay the bay leaves over the inside of one fillet and scatter over the fennel seeds. Lay the other fillet on top and tie up at 2.5 cm (1 inch) intervals with fine string. The fish should look like a long pork fillet.

3 With the tip of a sharp knife, make slits all over the monkfish and push in the garlic slivers. Pour the olive oil, thyme and a little ground black pepper into a glass dish and add the monkfish, turning well to coat. Cover and leave to marinate in the refrigerator for at least 2 hours, or preferably overnight.

4 Remove the fish from the marinade. Pour 2 tablespoons of the marinade into a heavy nonstick frying pan and heat until almost smoking. Add the monkfish and turn to seal for 2–3 minutes. Remove the fish and set aside.

5 In the same pan, heat the remaining marinade and quickly brown the peppers, aubergine and courgettes. Transfer the vegetables to a heavy shallow baking dish, set the monkfish on top and add the tomatoes and lemon juice. Bake in a preheated oven at 220°C (425°F), Gas Mark 7 for 20 minutes, basting occasionally and turning the vegetables from time to time.

6 Take the monkfish out of the oven and remove the string. Cut the fish into thick slices, discarding the bay leaves. Season the vegetables with salt and pepper to taste. Serve the monkfish on the roasted vegetable stew, garnished with chopped capers and parsley.

steamed whole fish

Serves 4 – Preparation time: 20 minutes – Cooking time: about 10 minutes

Per serving – 312 kcals/1304 kJ · Protein 35 g · Carbohydrate 5 g · Fat 17 g · Saturated fat 3 g · Fibre 0 g

2 x	**500 g (1 lb) sea bass or grey mullet, gutted**
5 cm	**(2 inch) piece of fresh root ginger, peeled and very thinly sliced**
6	**spring onions, very thinly sliced**
4	**garlic cloves, finely sliced**
6	**teaspoons sesame oil**
3	**heaped tablespoons canned salted black beans, rinsed**
3	**tablespoons groundnut oil**
2	**tablespoons rice wine or dry sherry**
2–3	**tablespoons chopped coriander leaves, to garnish**
	bean thread noodles, to serve

1 With a cleaver or sharp knife, make diagonal slashes on both sides of the fish, working right down to the bones. Place the two fish head to tail on a plate that will just fit inside a steamer. Insert the slices of ginger inside the fish and in the diagonal slashes, then sprinkle about half of the spring onions and garlic inside and over the fish. Drizzle each fish with 2 teaspoons of the sesame oil.

2 Put the plate of fish inside the steamer and cover with the lid. Steam over a high heat for 8 minutes, without lifting the lid.

3 Meanwhile, mash about two-thirds of the black beans, leaving the remainder whole. Heat the remaining sesame oil and the groundnut oil in a small wok or saucepan. Add the remaining spring onions and garlic, the mashed and whole black beans and the rice wine or sherry. Stir-fry over a high heat for a few minutes until sizzling.

4 Transfer the fish to a warmed serving platter. Pour any fish juices from the cooking plate into the black bean sauce, then spoon the sauce over the fish. Serve immediately with bean thread noodles, and garnished with coriander.

tuna steaks glazed with balsamic vinegar and basil oil

Serves 4 – Preparation time: 10 minutes, plus marinating – Cooking time: 8 minutes

Per serving – 369 kcals/1540 kJ · Protein 42 g · Carbohydrate 1 g · Fat 22 g · Saturated fat 4 g · Fibre 0 g

4 x	**175 g (6 oz) tuna steaks**
2	**tablespoons balsamic vinegar**
2	**teaspoons soy sauce**
75 ml	**(3 fl oz) extra virgin olive oil**
50 g	**(2 oz) basil leaves, plus extra to garnish**
	salt
	pepper

1 Place the tuna steaks in a shallow glass or ceramic dish. Mix together the balsamic vinegar and soy sauce and pour over the tuna steaks, turning them so they are thoroughly coated. Cover the dish and leave to marinate in the refrigerator for at least 30 minutes.

2 Pour the olive oil into a food processor or blender, add the basil and liquidize until smooth. Season with salt and pepper, pour into a bowl, cover and leave to infuse.

3 Preheat a grill or barbecue. Remove the tuna from the marinade and place on a foil-lined grill pan. Grill the steaks for about 4 minutes on each side, brushing with the marinade.

4 To serve, whisk the basil oil again then drizzle it over the steaks. Garnish with basil leaves.

monkfish in salsa d'agrumi

Serves 4 – Preparation time: 20 minutes – Cooking time: 10 minutes

Per serving – 215 kcals/906 kJ · Protein 28 g · Carbohydrate 6 g · Fat 6 g · Saturated fat 1 g · Fibre 0 g

875 g **(1¾ lb) monkfish**
flour, for coating
2 **tablespoons olive oil**
finely grated rind and juice of 1 lemon
finely grated rind and juice of 1 orange
150 ml **(¼ pint) dry white wine**
2 **tablespoons chopped parsley**
salt
pepper

To Garnish:
orange rind
parsley sprigs
orange and lemon wedges

1 Trim any membrane and dark meat from the monkfish. Remove the central bone by slitting the fish down the middle until you reach the bone. Turn the fish over and do the same on the other side. Ease out the bone, by gently scraping the flesh away with the tip of a knife. Cut the fish into large chunks and toss them in seasoned flour, shaking off the excess.

2 Heat the oil in a nonstick frying pan and fry the fish until golden all over. Remove the fish to a plate.

3 Add the lemon and orange rind and juice to the pan with the wine and boil rapidly to evaporate the alcohol. Turn down the heat, then return the fish to the pan and simmer gently for 3–4 minutes or until the fish is cooked. Stir in the parsley and salt and pepper to taste. Lift out the fish on to a warmed serving dish. Boil the sauce to reduce it a little more then pour over the fish. Serve immediately garnished with orange rind, parsley sprigs and orange and lemon wedges.

grilled squid with coriander noodles

Serves 4 – Preparation time: 15 minutes, plus soaking – Cooking time: 4–6 minutes

Per serving – 328 kcals/1380 kJ · Protein 25 g · Carbohydrate 44 g · Fat 6 g · Saturated fat 1 g · Fibre 3 g

475 g **(15 oz) prepared baby squid**
oil, for brushing
salt
pepper

Coriander Noodles:

200 g **(7 oz) flat rice noodles or medium**
egg noodles
1 **tablespoon light soy sauce or tamari**
1 **tablespoon lime juice**
2 **teaspoons Thai fish sauce**
1 **tablespoon clear honey**
4 **tablespoons roughly chopped**
coriander leaves
2 **tablespoons roughly chopped mint**
½ **red pepper, skinned, cored, deseeded**
and finely diced

1 Cut the squid in half lengthways and pat dry with kitchen paper. Use a sharp knife to score the inner surface of each piece in a criss-cross pattern, taking care not to cut right through. Arrange the squid on a grill rack and brush with oil. Sprinkle with salt and pepper and set aside.

2 Place the rice noodles in a large bowl and pour in enough boiling water to cover them. Leave to soak for 5 minutes, then drain and return the noodles to the bowl.

3 In a small bowl, mix the soy sauce or tamari, lime juice, fish sauce, honey, chopped coriander leaves, mint and diced red pepper. Add this mixture to the noodles and toss to mix well.

4 Place the squid under a preheated very hot grill and cook for 2–3 minutes on each side or until just cooked. While the squid is cooking, divide the noodles among 4 plates. Arrange the grilled squid on top of the noodles and serve at once.

roast cod with vegetables

Serves 4 – Preparation time: 5 minutes – Cooking time: 25 minutes

Per serving – 386 kcals/1620 kJ · Protein 37 g · Carbohydrate 28 g · Fat 14 g · Saturated fat 2 g · Fibre 6 g

750 g **(1½ lb) cod fillets, skinned**
4 **potatoes, quartered**
6 **tomatoes, halved**
1 **red onion, quartered**
1 **fennel bulb, cut into wedges**
2 **garlic cloves, chopped**
75 g **(3 oz) black olives, pitted**
25 g **(1 oz) green olives, pitted**
25 g **(1 oz) salted capers, rinsed**
4 **tablespoons lemon juice**
3 **tablespoons olive oil**
salt
pepper
handful of chopped parsley, to garnish

1 Put the cod, potatoes, tomatoes, onion and fennel into a large lightly oiled dish. Try to arrange them in a single layer. Sprinkle with the garlic, olives, capers and lemon juice and season with salt and pepper.

2 Drizzle with olive oil and place at the top of a preheated oven at 230°C (450°F), Gas Mark 8 and roast for 25 minutes.

3 Garnish with flat leaf parsley and serve immediately.

red mullet 'in cartoccio'

Serves 4 – Preparation time: 25 minutes – Cooking time: 20 minutes

Per serving – 297 kcals/1248 kJ · Protein 38 g · Carbohydrate 7 g · Fat 13 g · Saturated fat 1 g · Fibre 1 g

2 **tablespoons olive oil, plus extra for brushing**
2 **oranges**
8 **bay leaves**
4 x **250 g (8 oz) red mullet, scaled and gutted**
salt
pepper

1 Cut 4 rectangles of baking parchment or greaseproof paper big enough to loosely wrap a fish. Brush the rectangles with a little oil.

2 Grate the rind from the oranges, mix with the olive oil, season with salt and pepper and set aside. Peel the oranges, removing all the white pith. Slice them thinly. Place a bay leaf in the cavity of each fish and one on top.

3 Use half of the orange slices to make a row on one side of each parchment rectangle. Put the fish on the slices and cover them with the remaining orange slices. Drizzle with the oil and orange rind. Season well.

4 Fold the free paper loosely over the fish and twist the edges together to seal. Lift the packages on to a baking sheet and bake in a preheated oven at 190°C (375°F), Gas Mark 5 for 20 minutes. Serve immediately, opening the packages at the table.

monkfish kebabs with coriander, chilli and spring onion mash

Serves 4 – Preparation time: 30 minutes – Cooking time: about 25 minutes

Per serving – 320 kcals/1356 kJ · Protein 31 g · Carbohydrate 36 g · Fat 7 g · Saturated fat 4 g · Fibre 3 g

600 g	**(1 lb 3 oz) monkfish fillet, cut into 2.5 cm (1 inch) cubes**
125 ml	**(4 fl oz) low-fat natural yogurt**
1	**teaspoon crushed garlic**
1	**teaspoon grated fresh root ginger**
1	**teaspoon hot chilli powder**
1	**tablespoon ground coriander**
1	**tablespoon ground cumin**
	salt
	pepper

Coriander, Chilli and Spring Onion Mash:

6	**large Desirée or King Edward potatoes, diced**
150 ml	**(¼ pint) half-fat crème fraîche**
4	**tablespoons finely chopped coriander leaves**
1	**red chilli, deseeded and thinly sliced**
4	**spring onions, thinly sliced**

1 Lay the monkfish in a large, shallow ceramic or glass dish. In a small bowl, mix the yogurt, garlic, ginger, chilli powder, ground coriander and cumin. Season the mixture with salt and pepper and pour it over the fish. Cover and leave to marinate while you make the mash.

2 Bring a large saucepan of water to the boil. Add the potatoes, bring back to the boil and cook for 10 minutes, until tender. Drain the potatoes in a colander and return them to the pan.

3 Mash the potatoes and add the crème fraîche. Continue mashing until smooth and then stir in the chopped coriander leaves, sliced chilli and spring onions. Season to taste, cover and set aside.

4 Thread the cubes of fish on to 4 metal skewers and cook under a preheated very hot grill for 8–10 minutes, turning once. Serve immediately with the mash.

chicken, lemon and olive stew

Serves 4 – Preparation time: 15 minutes – Cooking time: about 1 hour

Per serving – 273 kcals/1140 kJ · Protein 34 g · Carbohydrate 3 g · Fat 14 g · Saturated fat 3 g · Fibre 2 g

2	tablespoons olive oil
4	skinless chicken breasts
12	baby onions, peeled
2	garlic cloves, crushed
1	teaspoon ground cumin
1	teaspoon ground ginger
1	teaspoon ground turmeric
½	teaspoon ground cinnamon
450 ml	(¾ pint) chicken stock
125 g	(4 oz) Kalamata olives
1	preserved lemon, chopped
2	tablespoons chopped coriander
	salt
	pepper
	plain boiled rice, to serve

1 Heat the oil in a flameproof casserole and brown the chicken breasts on all sides. Remove the chicken with a slotted spoon and set aside.

2 Add the onions, garlic and spices and sauté over a low heat for 10 minutes, until just golden. Return the chicken to the pan, stir in the stock and bring to the boil. Cover the casserole and simmer gently for 30 minutes.

3 Add the olives, chopped lemon and coriander and cook for a further 15–20 minutes until the chicken is really tender. Taste and adjust the seasoning and serve with rice.

pimento chicken

Serves 8 – Preparation time: 15 minutes, plus cooling – Cooking time: 1¾–2¼ hours

Per serving – 267 kcals/1123 kJ · Protein 38 g · Carbohydrate 8 g · Fat 10 g · Saturated fat 3 g · Fibre 1 g

2 kg	(4 lb) oven-ready chicken
1	onion, quartered
1	carrot, sliced
4	juniper berries, crushed
1	bay leaf
4–6	parsley stalks
	salt
6	peppercorns, lightly crushed
	griddled courgette slices, to serve (optional)
	chopped parsley, to garnish

Sauce:

250 g	(8 oz) canned pimentos, drained, rinsed and chopped
1	tablespoon tomato purée
2	tablespoons mango chutney
200 ml	(7 fl oz) low-fat natural yogurt
	salt
	pepper

1 Put the chicken, vegetables, juniper berries, bay leaf, parsley, salt and peppercorns into a saucepan. Cover with water. Bring to the boil, cover the saucepan and simmer for 1½–2 hours, or until the chicken is tender. Leave the chicken to cool in the stock. Lift out the chicken, drain and dry it. Reserve the stock, discarding the bay leaf. Skin the chicken and slice the meat from the bones.

2 To make the sauce, put the pimentos, 2 tablespoons of the reserved chicken stock, the tomato purée and chutney into a saucepan and bring to the boil. Transfer to a food processor or blender and blend until smooth. Set aside to cool. Blend the cooled pimento mixture with the yogurt and season with salt and pepper to taste.

3 Arrange the chicken on a serving dish and pour over the sauce. Garnish with parsley and serve with griddled courgettes, if liked.

chicken with ginger

Serves 4 – Preparation time: 20 minutes, plus marinating – Cooking time: about 6 minutes
Per serving – 173 kcals/729 kJ · Protein 22 g · Carbohydrate 7 g · Fat 6 g · Saturated fat 1 g · Fibre 2 g

375 g	(12 oz) boneless, skinless chicken breast
1	tablespoon dry sherry
4	spring onions, chopped
2	large carrots, thinly sliced
2.5 cm	(1 inch) piece of fresh root ginger, peeled and finely chopped
1	tablespoon oil
1–2	garlic cloves, thinly sliced
2	celery sticks, diagonally sliced
1	small green pepper, cored, deseeded and sliced
1	small yellow pepper, cored, deseeded and sliced
2	tablespoons light soy sauce
2	tablespoons lemon juice
	grated rind of 2 lemons
½	teaspoon chilli powder
	chives, to garnish

1 Cut the chicken into 7 cm (3 inch) strips. Combine the sherry, spring onions, carrots and ginger, add the chicken and toss well to coat, then set aside for 15 minutes.

2 Heat the oil in a large nonstick frying pan or wok. Add the garlic, celery and green and yellow peppers and stir fry for 1 minute. Add the chicken and marinade and cook for 3 minutes. Stir in the soy sauce, lemon juice and rind and chilli powder and cook for a further 1 minute.

3 Divide between 4 warmed serving plates and serve immediately, garnished with chives.

sweet and sour chinese turkey

Serves 4 – Preparation time: 15 minutes, plus marinating – Cooking time: 8 minutes
Per serving – 247 kcals/1042 kJ · Protein 31 g · Carbohydrate 14 g · Fat 8 g · Saturated fat 1 g · Fibre 2 g

500 g	(1 lb) boneless, skinless turkey breast
2	tablespoons lemon juice
5	tablespoons orange juice
4	celery sticks
2	sharon fruit or firm tomatoes
8–10	radishes
½	Chinese cabbage
1	large green pepper, cored and deseeded
2	tablespoons oil
150 ml	(¼ pint) chicken stock
1½	teaspoons cornflour
1	tablespoon soy sauce
1	tablespoon clear honey
	boiled rice, to serve (optional)
	orange rind, to garnish

1 Cut the turkey breast into thin strips and marinate in the lemon and orange juices for 30 minutes. Cut the celery, sharon fruit or tomatoes, radishes, Chinese cabbage and green pepper into small neat pieces.

2 Heat the oil in a large nonstick frying pan or wok. Drain the turkey and reserve the marinade. Fry the turkey in the oil until nearly cooked. Add the vegetables and sharon fruit or tomatoes and cook for 2–3 minutes.

3 Blend the chicken stock with the marinade and the cornflour. Add the soy sauce and honey. Pour this mixture over the ingredients in the pan and stir until thickened. Serve immediately with boiled rice, if liked, and garnished with orange rind.

bonbonji

Serves 4 – Preparation time: 30 minutes, plus chilling – Cooking time: about 20 minutes

Per serving – 172 kcals/720 kJ · Protein 24 g · Carbohydrate 2 g · Fat 8 g · Saturated fat 2 g · Fibre 0 g

2   **spring onions, roughly chopped**
2   **part-boned chicken breasts**
    about 300 ml (½ pint) chicken stock
7.5 cm **(3 inch) piece of cucumber**
    salt
    pepper
    toasted sesame seeds, to garnish

Dressing:
1   **tablespoon sesame paste**
1   **tablespoon light soy sauce**
2   **teaspoons rice wine vinegar, white**
    wine vinegar or cider vinegar
    a few drops of chilli oil or 1 teaspoon
    chilli sauce
1   **teaspoon sugar**

1 Put the spring onions into a wok, then lay the chicken breasts skin side down on top of them and season with salt and pepper. Cover the chicken with stock and bring to a gentle simmer, then cover the pan with a lid and poach very gently for 15 minutes, turning once.

2 Remove the chicken from the stock, reserving the stock, and place it skin side up on a board. With a rolling pin, pound the chicken to loosen the skin and fibres. Leave until it is cool enough to handle.

3 Remove and discard the skin and bones from the chicken, then thinly shred the meat with your fingers. Cut the cucumber into matchsticks, discarding the seeds and as much skin as you like. Arrange the pieces of chicken and cucumber on a serving dish.

4 Put all the dressing ingredients into a food processor and add 4 tablespoons of the poaching liquid (skimmed to remove the fat). Process until all the ingredients are evenly mixed, then taste and add more chilli oil or chilli sauce if liked. Spoon the dressing over the chicken and cucumber, cover and chill in the refrigerator for about 4 hours. Serve sprinkled with the toasted sesame seeds.

japanese rice with nori

Serves 4 – Preparation time: 10 minutes – Cooking time: 15 minutes

Per serving – 296 kcals/1237 kJ · Protein 10 g · Carbohydrate 46 g · Fat 7 g · Saturated fat 1 g · Fibre 3 g

225 g	**(7½ oz) Japanese sushi or glutinous rice**
400 ml	**(14 fl oz) water**
2	**tablespoons black or white sesame seeds**
1	**teaspoon coarse salt**
1	**tablespoon groundnut or vegetable oil**
2	**eggs, beaten**
4	**spring onions, finely sliced**
1	**red chilli, deseeded and sliced**
4	**tablespoons seasoned rice vinegar**
2	**teaspoons caster sugar**
1	**tablespoon light soy sauce**
25 g	**(1 oz) pickled Japanese ginger**
2	**sheets of roasted nori seaweed**

1 Place the rice in a heavy-based saucepan with the water. Bring to the boil, then reduce the heat and simmer, uncovered, for about 5 minutes until all the water is absorbed. Cover the pan and cook for a further 5 minutes until the rice is cooked.

2 Meanwhile, place the sesame seeds in a small frying pan with the salt and heat gently for about 2 minutes until the seeds are lightly toasted. Remove from the pan and set aside.

3 Heat the oil in the pan, add the beaten eggs and cook gently until just firm. Slide the omelette on to a plate, roll up and cut across into shreds.

4 Transfer the cooked rice to a bowl and stir in the spring onions, chilli, rice vinegar, sugar, soy sauce, ginger and half the toasted sesame seeds. Crumble one sheet of nori over the rice and stir in with the omelette shreds.

5 Transfer to a serving dish. Crumble the remaining nori over the rice and scatter with the remaining toasted sesame seeds.

bulgar wheat salad

Serves 4 – Preparation time: 20 minutes, plus standing

Per serving – 329 kcals/1367 kJ · Protein 5 g · Carbohydrate 39 g · Fat 18 g · Saturated fat 2 g · Fibre 1 g

175 g	(6 oz) bulgar wheat
1	red onion, finely chopped
2	ripe tomatoes, finely chopped
½	cucumber, diced
1	garlic clove, crushed
1	small red chilli, deseeded and finely chopped
4	tablespoons chopped parsley
2	tablespoons chopped mint
2	tablespoons chopped coriander
2	tablespoons lemon juice
6	tablespoons extra virgin olive oil
	salt
	pepper

1 Put the bulgar wheat into a large bowl and cover with boiling water. Leave to soak for 30 minutes, then drain off the excess water.

2 Stir in all the remaining ingredients and season to taste with salt and pepper. Cover and set aside to infuse for at least 30 minutes, for the flavours to develop.

green couscous with spiced fruit sauce

Serves 4 – Preparation time: 15 minutes – Cooking time: 15 minutes

Per serving – 385 kcals/1615 kJ · Protein 13 g · Carbohydrate 47 g · Fat 17 g · Saturated fat 1 g · Fibre 10 g

250 g	(8 oz) couscous
500 ml	(17 fl oz) hot vegetable stock
75 g	(3 oz) unsalted, shelled pistachio nuts, roughly chopped
2	spring onions, chopped
	small handful of parsley, chopped
425 g	(14 oz) can flageolet beans, rinsed and drained
½	teaspoon saffron threads
1	tablespoon cardamom pods
2	teaspoons coriander seeds
½	teaspoon chilli powder
4	tablespoons flaked almonds
73 g	(3 oz) ready-to-eat dried apricots
	salt
	pepper

1 Place the couscous in a bowl. Add 300 ml (½ pint) of the hot stock. Leave to stand for 5 minutes until the stock is absorbed, then stir in the pistachio nuts, spring onions, parsley and beans and season with salt and pepper. Cover with a lid or foil and place in a preheated oven at 150°C (300°F), Gas Mark 2 for 15 minutes.

2 Meanwhile, place the saffron in a small cup with 1 tablespoon of boiling water and leave for 3 minutes. Crush the cardamom pods using a pestle and mortar or the end of a rolling pin. Pick out and discard the pods then lightly crush the seeds.

3 Transfer the cardamom seeds to a food processor or blender with the coriander seeds, chilli powder, almonds and apricots. Process until finely chopped. Add the saffron and soaking liquid, the remaining stock and salt and pepper and blend until pulpy. Transfer to a saucepan and heat through for 1 minute. Serve with the couscous.

saffron-spiced vegetable couscous

Serves 6 – Preparation time: 20 minutes, plus soaking – Cooking time: about 1 hour

Per serving – 358 kcals/1498 kJ · Protein 10 g · Carbohydrate 62 g · Fat 10 g · Saturated fat 3 g · Fibre 5 g

475 g	(15 oz) couscous
300 ml	(½ pint) water
250 g	(8 oz) carrots, cut into chunks
250 g	(8 oz) turnips, cut into chunks
1–2	large fennel bulbs, each cut into 6 wedges
1	large aubergine, cubed
250 g	(8 oz) courgettes, thickly sliced
25 g	(1 oz) butter
2–3	tablespoons finely chopped coriander leaves
	salt
	coriander sprigs, to garnish

Sweet Spicy Sauce:

2	tablespoons extra virgin olive oil
2	large onions, cut into wedges
4	garlic cloves, crushed
2.5 cm	(1 inch) piece of fresh root ginger, peeled and grated
1	tablespoon ground cumin
1	tablespoon ground coriander
1	teaspoon turmeric
1	teaspoon paprika
1	teaspoon black pepper
5 cm	(2 inch) cinnamon stick
1	teaspoon saffron threads, soaked in 2 tablespoons warm water
750 ml	(1¼ pints) vegetable stock
2 x	400 g (13 oz) cans chopped tomatoes
2	tablespoons tomato purée
2	tablespoons sweet chilli sauce

1 Put the couscous into a bowl, cover with the water and leave to soak for 10 minutes. Fork through and leave for a further 10 minutes.

2 Meanwhile, prepare the sauce. Heat 1 tablespoon of the oil in a large saucepan. Fry the onions until beginning to brown, then add the garlic and ginger. Stir in the ground spices and cinnamon stick and fry for a few minutes. Add the soaked saffron to the pan with the stock, tomatoes, tomato purée and chilli sauce. Bring to the boil. Add the carrots and turnips to the sauce, reduce the heat, cover and cook for about 10 minutes.

3 Heat the remaining oil in a large frying pan and fry the fennel wedges until lightly coloured. Transfer to the sauce with a slotted spoon. Fry the aubergine and courgettes until browned, adding a little extra oil if necessary. Drain and add to the sauce. Cook gently for 15–20 minutes until the vegetables are tender and the sauce is rich and thick. During this final cooking, steam the couscous according to packet instructions.

4 To serve, pile the couscous in a large dish, fleck with pieces of butter and stir in with a fork. Stir the chopped coriander into the stew and add salt to taste. Serve a mound of couscous to each person, spoon the vegetable stew on top and garnish with coriander sprigs.

warm chickpea salad

Serves 4 – Preparation time: 10 minutes – Cooking time: 10 minutes

Per serving – 370 kcals/1554 kJ · Protein 15 g · Carbohydrate 36 g · Fat 20 g · Saturated fat 3 g · Fibre 9 g

5	tablespoons extra virgin olive oil
1	red onion, finely chopped
2	garlic cloves, crushed
4 cm	(1½ inch) piece of fresh root ginger, peeled and grated
2 x	400 g (13 oz) cans chickpeas, drained
	pinch of dried chilli flakes
	juice and finely grated rind of 1½ lemons
1	bunch of coriander, chopped
	salt
	pepper
	mixed ground cumin and paprika, to garnish

1 Heat 1 tablespoon of the oil in a frying pan. Add the onion, garlic and ginger and cook gently for 5–7 minutes, stirring occasionally, until soft and translucent.

2 Add the chickpeas, chilli flakes and lemon rind and stir for about 30 seconds, then add the lemon juice and let the mixture bubble until it is almost dry. Add the coriander and season to taste with salt and pepper.

3 Transfer the mixture to a serving dish, pour over the remaining olive oil and set aside to cool. Serve warm, sprinkled with a little ground cumin and paprika.

italian bean casserole

Serves 4 – Preparation time: 15 minutes, plus soaking – Cooking time: 2 hours

Per serving – 366 kcals/1550 kJ · Protein 22 g · Carbohydrate 57 g · Fat 7 g · Saturated fat 1 g · Fibre 8 g

125 g	(4 oz) red kidney beans, soaked in cold water overnight
125 g	(4 oz) cannellini beans, soaked in cold water overnight
125 g	(4 oz) flageolet beans, soaked in cold water overnight
2	tablespoons olive oil
1	onion, chopped
1	green pepper, cored, deseeded and chopped
1	teaspoon dried oregano
150 g	(5 oz) tomato purée
300 ml	(½ pint) water
1	teaspoon caster sugar
	salt
	pepper
	oregano or marjoram sprigs, to garnish

1 Cook the beans separately to avoid the red beans colouring the others. Cover with cold water, bring to the boil and boil rapidly for 10 minutes, then reduce the heat and simmer until the beans are just tender.

2 Heat the oil in a heavy-based frying pan. Add the onion and green pepper and fry over a medium heat, stirring occasionally, for about 5 minutes until softened.

3 Add the oregano, tomato purée, water and sugar, and season to taste with salt and pepper. Bring to the boil.

4 Drain the beans, put them into a casserole and pour the onion and pepper sauce over them. Cook uncovered in a preheated oven at 160°C (325°F), Gas Mark 3 for 1 hour, stirring frequently but gently until most of the liquid has been absorbed. Serve hot, garnished with oregano or marjoram sprigs.

jewelled tabbouleh

Serves 4 – Preparation time: 15 minutes – Cooking time: about 20 minutes

Per serving – 490 kcals/2044 kJ · Protein 11 g · Carbohydrate 72 g · Fat 19 g · Saturated fat 2 g · Fibre 5 g

3	tablespoons olive oil
1	large onion, roughly chopped
300 g	(10 oz) bulgar wheat
750 ml	(1½ pints) vegetable stock
50 g	(2 oz) pine nuts, toasted
4	dried apricots, roughly chopped
	seeds from 1 small pomegranate
4	tablespoons roughly chopped mint
1	tablespoon lemon juice
	salt
	pepper
	mint leaves, to garnish

1   Heat 1 tablespoon of the oil in a saucepan, add the onion and cook briskly, stirring often, until it is soft. Add the bulgar wheat and the stock and bring to the boil. Cover the pan, reduce the heat and simmer gently for 15 minutes, stirring occasionally, or until the stock is absorbed and the wheat is tender.

2   Turn the bulgar wheat into a large serving bowl. Mix in the pine nuts, apricots, pomegranate seeds and chopped mint.

3   In a small bowl, mix the remaining oil with the lemon juice, then pour this dressing over the wheat mixture. Season to taste and toss until well mixed. Garnish with mint leaves and serve immediately.

apricot and banana compôte

Serves 4 – Preparation time: 15 minutes, plus soaking and chilling

Per serving – 144 kcals/614 kJ · Protein 4 g · Carbohydrate 32 g · Fat 1 g · Saturated fat 0 g · Fibre 9 g

125 g	**(4 oz) dried apricots**
2	**bananas**
2	**teaspoons lemon juice**
25 g	**(1 oz) raisins**
150 ml	**(¼ pint) low-fat natural yogurt**
	clear honey, to taste (optional)
	grated nutmeg

1 Wash the apricots, place in a bowl and cover with cold water. Leave to soak overnight.

2 Slice the bananas and toss in the lemon juice. Place the apricots in a bowl with a little of the soaking liquid. Add the bananas and raisins, then divide the fruit between 4 serving dishes.

3 Sweeten the yogurt with honey, if liked, spoon over the fruit and sprinkle with grated nutmeg. Chill before serving.

baked cranberry pears

Serves 4 – Preparation time: 20 minutes – Cooking time: 40 minutes

Per serving – 200 kcals/848 kJ · Protein 2 g · Carbohydrate 41 g · Fat 2 g · Saturated fat 0 g · Fibre 3 g

4	large, ripe dessert pears, peeled but with the stalks intact
250 g	(8 oz) cranberries, thawed if frozen
1	tablespoon chopped hazelnuts
3	tablespoons clear honey
150 ml	(¼ pint) dry white wine
	mint sprigs, to decorate

1 Working from the base and using a small teaspoon, scoop out the pear cores. Chop 2 tablespoons of the cranberries and mix with the nuts and 1 tablespoon of the honey. Press the mixture into the pear cavities.

2 Put the remaining cranberries and honey and the wine into a flameproof dish and bring to the boil over a moderate heat. Simmer for 5 minutes. Stand the pears upright in the dish and spoon the wine over them.

3 Cover the dish lightly with foil and cook in a preheated oven at 200°C (400°F), Gas Mark 6 for 30 minutes, basting the pears with the wine once or twice. Serve hot or cold, decorated with mint sprigs.

exotic fruit salad

Serves 4 – Preparation time: 30 minutes, plus chilling – Cooking time: 5 minutes
Per serving – 224 kcals/954 kJ · Protein 3 g · Carbohydrate 54 g · Fat 1 g · Saturated fat 0 g · Fibre 7 g

2	**tablespoons clear honey**
125 ml	**(4 fl oz) water**
	thinly pared rind and juice of 1 lemon
2	**bananas**
1	**small pineapple**
2	**oranges**
2	**kiwi fruits, peeled and thinly sliced**
1	**mango, peeled, pitted and cubed**
125 g	**(4 oz) strawberries, hulled and halved**
1	**small Charentais or Galia melon, peeled and cubed**
	ground cinnamon
	mint sprigs, to decorate

1 Place the honey, water and lemon rind in a small pan. Bring to the boil over a low heat, simmer for 2 minutes, then strain and set aside to cool. Stir in the lemon juice.

2 Slice the bananas into diagonal slices and place in a bowl. Pour over the lemon syrup and stir to coat the fruit completely.

3 Peel the pineapple, remove the eyes and cut the flesh into sections, discarding the central core.

4 Peel the oranges, removing all the pith, and divide into segments. Add to the bowl with the pineapple, kiwi, mango, strawberries and melon. Mix carefully, but thoroughly. Chill until required, then sprinkle with cinnamon and decorate with mint sprigs.

fragrant fruit salad

Serves 6 – Preparation time: 30 minutes, plus chilling – Cooking time: 3–4 minutes

Per serving – 145 kcals/620 kJ · Protein 1 g · Carbohydrate 34 g · Fat 0 g · Saturated fat 0 g · Fibre 3 g

75 g	(3 oz) sugar
2	pieces of star anise
1	cinnamon stick
200 ml	(7 fl oz) cold water
1	ripe pineapple
2	ripe mangoes
250 g	(8 oz) lychees
4	tablespoons Chinese rice wine or dry sherry

To Decorate:
star anise
cape gooseberries (physalis)
pineapple leaves

1 Put the sugar, star anise and cinnamon stick into a heavy saucepan and pour in the cold water. Heat gently until the sugar has dissolved, then boil for 2 minutes. Remove from the heat, cover the pan and leave to cool.

2 Meanwhile, prepare the fruit. Peel the pineapple, remove the eyes and cut the flesh into sections, discarding the central core. Peel and chop the mangoes and peel and stone the lychees.

3 Put the fruit into a large bowl, strain the sugar syrup over it and add the rice wine or sherry. Stir gently to mix. Cover and chill for at least 4 hours. Before serving, decorate with whole star anise, cape gooseberries and pineapple leaves.

glossary

ADRENALINE (EPINEPHRINE):
A hormone released in response to activity or stress which increases the heart rate.

ANGINA:
Chest pain caused by atherosclerosis of the coronary arteries.

ANGIOGRAM:
A moving X-ray of the coronary arteries and other parts of the heart.

AORTA:
The body's main artery.

ARTERIOLES:
Small arteries supplying the body's organs.

ATHEROMA:
A substance that builds up in the arteries leading to atherosclerosis.

ATHEROSCLEROSIS:
Furring and hardening of the arteries caused by a build-up of atheroma.

ATRIUM:
One of the two upper chambers of the heart which receive blood into the heart.

CAPILLARIES:
The smallest blood vessels with walls one cell thick through which oxygen and carbon dioxide are exchanged.

CARDIAC CATHETERIZATION:
Insertion of a small tube via a vein or artery in the groin or arm to allow a coronary angiogram to be performed.

CARDIAC CENTRE:
A cluster of cells in the brain which automatically controls the action of the heart.

CARDIAC CYCLE:
The two-phase cycle that makes up one heartbeat.

CARDIAC OUTPUT:
The amount of blood pumped out with each heartbeat.

CARDIOVASCULAR SYSTEM:
The system comprising the heart and the blood vessels.

CHOLESTEROL:
A fatty substance made in the liver which contributes to heart disease.

CONDUCTION:
The system of electrical timing that controls the cardiac cycle.

CORONARY ANGIOPLASTY:
A procedure to open up narrowed arteries using a 'balloon' or a stent.

CORONARY ARTERIES:
The arteries which arise from the aorta and supply the heart with oxygen and nutrients.

CORONARY BYPASS:
An operation to bypass narrowed sections of arteries using a grafted blood vessel.

DIASTOLE:
The resting phase of the cardiac cycle when the heart fills with blood.

ENDOCARDIUM:
Smooth membrane lining the inside of the heart.

EPIDEMIOLOGY:
The study of patterns of disease in populations.

FAMILIAL HYPERCHO-LESTEROLAEMIA:
An inherited condition in which blood cholesterol levels are high, leading to increased risk of heart disease.

FIBRINOGEN:
A protein involved in blood clotting which seems to be a risk factor for heart disease.

FREE RADICALS:
Harmful molecules which damage cells and cause oxidation in the body.

HDL:
High-density lipoprotein, also known as 'good cholesterol'.

HOMOCYSTEINE:
An amino acid (protein-building block) which seems to be a risk factor for heart disease.

HYPERTENSION:
High blood pressure.

INSULIN RESISTANCE:
The body produces insulin but is unable to use it properly with the result that high levels of blood glucose develop in the bloodstream.

INTERMITTENT CLAUDICATION:
Pain in the legs resulting from peripheral vascular disease.

ISCHAEMIA:
When muscles are starved of oxygen as a result of atherosclerosis.

LDL:
Low-density lipoprotein, also known as 'bad cholesterol'.

LIPOPROTEINS:
Special carrier proteins which carry
cholesterol in the blood.

**MYOCARDIAL
INFARCTION:**
A heart attack, when the heart muscle
is deprived of oxygen and dies to be
replaced by scar tissue.

MYOCARDIUM:
The special type of muscle that the
heart walls are made of.

PACEMAKER:
The sinoatrial node, a bundle of cells
which transmits electrical impulses to
the atria, causing them to contract.

PERICARDIUM:
Tough, fibrous bag enclosing the
heart.

**PERIPHERAL
VASCULAR DISEASE
(PVD):**
A condition that occurs when the blood
supply to the legs is affected by
atherosclerosis.

PLAQUES:
Raised patches on the artery wall
composed of atheroma, which narrow
the artery.

PLATELETS:
Small blood cells involved in clotting.

**PULMONARY
CIRCUIT:**
The blood system serving the lungs.

REVASCULARIZATION:
A surgical procedure to open or
replace narrowed or blocked arteries.

SEPTUM:
Wall of muscle separating the right
and left sides of the heart.

STENT:
A short stainless-steel mesh tube
used in angioplasty to hold a blood
vessel open.

SYSTEMIC CIRCUIT:
The blood system serving the rest of
the body other than the lungs.

SYSTOLE:
The active phase of the cardiac cycle
when blood is pumped out of the
heart.

THROMBOSIS:
A blood clot blocking an artery.

**TRANSIENT
ISCHAEMIC ATTACK
(TIA):**
A mini-stroke that occurs when the
brain is briefly deprived of blood.

VENAE CAVA:
The body's main veins.

VENTRICLE:
One of the two lower chambers of
the heart which pump blood out
of the heart.

VENULES:
Small veins which join to form
larger veins.

glossary

125

index

index

Corbis UK Ltd
/Owen Franken 58 right

Octopus Publishing Group Ltd.
/Jean Cazals 62 bottom, 66
/Peter Chadwick 61
/Sandra Lane 5 bottom centre, 64, 69, 71 left, 71 right, 72 left
/David Loftus 5 bottom, 74–75, 83, 93
/James Merrell 68 bottom
/Neil Mersh 81, 82, 92, 97, 104, 106, 107, 116, 119, 120, 121
/Peter Myers 57
/Bill Reavell 76, 80, 87, 88, 114
/Simon Smith 3 bottom right, 84, 86, 98, 111, 112, 117, 118, 122
/Ian Wallace 1, 60 bottom, 67 top, 78, 89, 90, 91, 94, 95, 96, 100, 101, 102, 103, 105, 108, 113, 123

Image Bank
/Romilly Lockyer 72 right

Photodisc
2–3 bottom left, 26, 33 right, 37 bottom

Science Photo Library
10 bottom
/Paul Biddle 62 right
/Martyn F Chillmaid 44 top, 48, 50, 52 top
/John Greim 44 bottom
/P Hattenberger 5 top centre, 54, 56, 58 left, 60 top, 62 top left
/Mehau Kulyk 52 bottom
/Damien Lovegrove 23, 59
/Chris Priest 18
/Prof. P Motta/G Macchiarelli/University 'La Sparenza' Rome 16
/BSIP LECA 53
/St Bartholomew's Hospital, London 22
/Bo Vetsland 13

Stone
/Paul Arthur 24
/Bruce Ayres 20
/Steve Casimiro 39
/Martyn F Chillmaid 5 top, 42
/Steward Cohen 41
/Joe Cornish 68 top
/David Harry Steward 37 top
/Donna Day 29
/Nick Dolding 4 top centre, 8, 10 top, 12 top
/Ben Edwards 25
/Charles Gupton 49
/Chris Harvey 7 left
/David Madison 2–3 top, 11
/Jeff Mermelstein 27
/Sue Ann Miller 6
/Joe Polillio 4 top, 7 right
/Jon Riley 67 bottom
/Jed & Kaoru Share 63
/Charles Thatcher 4 bottom centre, 14
/Bob Thomas 4 bottom, 30, 32, 34, 36, 38, 40
/Penny Tweedie 12 bottom
/Caroline Wood 33 left

Wellcome Institute Library, London
19

Safety Note

Food Solutions: Healthy Heart should not be considered a replacement for professional medical treatment; a physician should be consulted in all matters relating to health, particularly in respect of pregnancy and any other symptoms which may require diagnosis or medical attention. While the advice and information in this book is believed to be accurate, neither the author nor publisher can accept any legal responsibility for any injury or illness sustained while following the treatments and diet plan.